YIEDLING 2 TEMPTATION

PART: 1

BY

T. A. ROBINSON

Yielding (2) Temptations

DEDICATION

To my eldest son Anthony Goffe, with an inflated chest and a proud heart I thank God for the man you have become. You give me so much joy knowing you have begun to achieve what you initially thought was the impossible. Your belief in accepting the opportunities given to you through hard work and determination, has now flourished into you having a bright future. It is through this ordeal and given opportunity in life (to see my children blossom in a world that could easily consume,) why I am so driven. I thank you my Son because you have turned out to be the man that has surpassed my high expectation. My hope is for you to continue to follow in your own good judgment and intellect of your own wisdom because I know that if you continue on this path of integrity, you will reap the rewards of success. I love you Son!

To Chantelle; mother of Alyssa and Kerah, I have only complete admiration for your determination and drive in raising your children as a single mother. To have dreams and ambitions with a merciless attitude of forging ahead with constructive plans, is a testament to your belief in giving your children the very best in life. Contributing love, not as a gift that is unwrapped on good days but, exercising love every moment even, when you are exhausted is an exemplary attribute to your fine quality of motherhood. Please continue in this strand of hope and I am sure your work will be greatly rewarded in the fullness of time.

To Daniel Robinson; over the years I've watched you grow into a fine young man that is self expressive and vibrant in personality. Even to this day I am constantly impressed by your rational methodical reasoning about life and how you relate to people around you. You are a proud, loving and responsible father which, in your devotion to your family and close acquaintances is greatly manifested with reciprocal evidence. I am proud of you Son and the individual determination to succeed in private entrepreneurial-ship is unreservedly admirable.

To Angelou Jeffers; The constant devotion to details in doing the things you know in your heart to be right is paramount in every aspect of your decision making. Your drive to succeed to advance yourself in the academic world is a

Yielding (2) Temptations

remarkable trait of insight and achieving the desired targeted goal of passing; will undoubtedly strengthen your visionary perceptions of future accomplishment. With youth and vivacity at your disposal, you will undoubtedly conquer everything you set your mind to do and do it with distinction. I believe in your ability Angelou to win the fight of consummate freedom and I am with you in whatever decision you take to make it all happen, successfully!

To Shanice Robinson; Life is like a rose whose stem is strengthened by the winds. The natural floatation of life's options bewilders the flower to lean in its direction. The selections of a career path resemble a junction that tailors off into different directions, hence; the choices we make, determined the outcome of our destiny. Shan, you are at a tender stage of development and the choices you make will lead you to a path of reality that no one else can walk with you. Your dreams and aspirations will be realised even if you make a mistake. Trust in your instincts Shanice and believe in yourself, the moment you feel you're alone, please remember; I am proud of you and will always be with you in whatever you do.

To Shola Robinson Jeffers; the unmistakable ability to acquire encouragement from the things around you will stand you in good stead for the future. The twilight years of darkened past is over and the dawn of a new era has now materialised into reality. Embrace the change with open arms Shola and free your mind in the preparation for the pleasantries that life has in store. Think carefully on the options you will have in your life because in these options, lay gems of opportunity just for you to raise them from under the rocks of possibility. Whatever the decisions you choose to make, always remember, I'm proud of the person you are.

To my Mother, Miss Gloria Robinson; you have been a tower of strength over the many years. Encouraging me to hold on when everything around me seemed to have failed. You believed that better days were always ahead of me and you lifted my spirits when disappointment showed its ugly face. I publicly declare to the world that I cherish every moment with you knowing that I can pick up the phone or spend quality time in person with you. May the good Lord continue to Bless and Keep You Safe and the love that is in my heart for you will Never Die but remain forever. Stay true to yourself Mum, always stay true to God and always remember you have a Son that will always have you in a secret place in his heart.

To Carol Johnson; "CJ," you have been a very close friend and confidant in my past and the present loyalty in our friendship will always remain. I owe my gratitude to you for recognizing my ability even when it wasn't clear to me. You have helped me on a journey that is more fulfilling than I could ever have imagined. I pray that you will continue to love the Lord with all your heart, and forever lean on his everlasting arms, with the assurance that your future is blessed with the ingredients of everlasting peace. Thank you.

And last but by-no-means least; My Grandmother; **Mrs Cynthia Ina Thompson**; If there was a single entity that demonstrates strength, honour, respect, reverence and encapsulated characteristics of a mother, father, brother, sister or friend, it would all be enveloped in this remarkable lady. Growing up in the early seventies, I was raised in an era where nothing was ever hidden from your parents. From smashing the glass on the garden shed to stealing the ice-lolly from the cooler, I never once during my adolescent period got away with anything. I was taught to wash, cook, clean and do all the essential amenities expected from an adult even as a little child. She taught me to read the Bible and preach it to her into the wee-hours of the morning and to go selling undergarments to grown woman who were sympathetic to my cause. It was an immense experience and it taught me from a very early age to be responsible. The discipline and dedication to produce this book was based on the foundation of executing a routine. A discipline I would never change for the world. If this was a platform to declare to the world that my first mother in life was my grandmother; I wouldn't be doing any injustice to my mother to say that, without my grandmother, I would be a completely different person from the person I am today. So kudos to You Gran; with utmost respect and reverence; I owe my life to you. Thank You Gran!

Yielding (2) Temptations

CONTENTS

DEDICATION   Pg   2

INTRODUCTION   Pg   6

Scene 1   Pg   8

Scene 2   Pg   28

Scene 3   Pg   51

Scene 4   Pg   67

Scene 5   Pg   81

Scene 6   Pg   96

Scene 7   Pg   112

Scene 8   Pg   134

Scene 9   Pg   157

Yielding (2) Temptations

Introduction

Yielding 2 Temptation

Volume 1

An eternal love is an inexpressible sentiment that is often misunderstood in various circumstances of life. But the underlying emotion behind the concept is sometimes mistakenly overlooked by the people, who in truth, desire it the most. The evidence is usually there for all to see, however; finding the secret ingredient that identifies the composition of a perfect match, at times is elusive to the trained eye. I believe we need to search the innermost parts of our heart and pacifying the reasoning for our choice is only the first step before we choose our supposed "Soul Mate." We are always certain from the foundation of any relationship that we made the right judgment, purely because our intelligence is clouded in a delusional state of desire. Selecting a particular partner of interest varies from person to person, hence the complexity levels in our matches are often compromised in the areas we wouldn't normally want them to be. We need to decide from an early stage what our priorities are, and executing them with the truthfulness that they deserve, requires meticulous honesty. A long lasting relationship that involves an unreserved devotion of truth and unyielding love must start from an immovable commitment that is unquestionable in the eyes of the beholder. There can be no questions unanswered when you are dealing with the absolute truth, the two hearts merging together for life's union will see the benefits, if they can only be truthful to one-another from the start.

Yielding (2) Temptations

Yielding 2 Temptation depicts some scenarios that could accumulate when desire is greater than reality. However, the feelings are real and should not be discounted because of the reality of hope being a mere impossibility.

A virtuous woman unintentionally falls in love with a preacher who is admired by all the females around him. Although older in age and more circumspect with her expression of feelings; her emotions at fragile moments, run into overdrive and are then discovered.

Never discount the power of love. Her dreams may seem impossible in reality but when she uses the source, the untapped energy that governs the order of life itself; then there is hope for her yet!

Thank you for spending time with me in reading!

T A Robinson

Author

Yielding (2) Temptations

Yielding (2) Temptations

Scene 1

The room was filled with the sweet essence and domineering character of masculine power, he captivated the hearts and minds of the wondering Christian souls of the theologically educated. The voice echoed through the room; as "Victoria" heard him say the most intriguing and motivating things. He consumed the table with a finesse and style, that, "V" (as she was known to all who knew her) had personally never seen before, he uttered each word with complete Perfection; his congregation were in a trance, male and female alike. The room was eerily quiet, as each anticipated his next syllable and phrase for their dessert and appetite; he soothingly steered each heart to the love of God and his Power. If he only knew, the impact he was having on her heart; If only he knew how "V"'s body was reacting to his words of Power and Anointing; She was lost in his effortless words of wisdom. What a man!

His eyes were now upon her! Her heart screamed out in fear! She focused hard because her eyes wanted to betray her true feeling for this gentleman of a man. His voice carried away "V"s sensual feelings of inner emotions, casting away momentarily her inhibition of her inner sensual emotions. He nodded his head in her direction, and smiled at her, willing her to verbally interject her opinion. She pulled herself together and re-adjusted her garment to illustrate that she was still in complete control and that his charm hadn't fazed her. It was time

Yielding (2) Temptations

for her to respond.

"V" knew all eyes were upon her, and she could not allow the staring to continue, her reputation, her self-respect was at stake and now everyone was now looking at her as if they expected that she had something to say. It was obvious she was going to have a dialogue with him, one-2-one. "V" prayed in her heart for God to give her the appropriate answer.

Victoria closed her eyes, she didn't remember how long she had been mentally praying because when she had closed her eyes she had shut the world out of her mind and focused on God. But as she opened up her eyes, everyone was staring hard, because this gentleman thought she was so caught up in what he was saying; he closed his eyes also and demanded that everybody in the room do the same, and then he asked her to pray. "V" was so captivated in her own little world she didn't hear a thing that he said to her, until the Pastor tugged at "V"'s blouse in frustration; as they couldn't wait any longer in the shame of her absentmindedness.

"V" opened one-eye and looked, and realised it was time to really start praying. Certain questions raced through her mind as she frantically tried to search for a good topic to pray for. She opened the prayer in standard procedural format, something that all Christians are able to do with little effort. This gave "V" the excellent chance to mentally surf the Christian Prayer Webb for a clue and hopefully find some answers, and then, she got it! Current affairs and disasters, as she was sure the young man mentioned something about a disaster in Asia. "V" realised she was coming to the inspirational zone of her prayer; she was almost completing her standard

Yielding (2) Temptations

format intro, and now realising that it was time to now go for it.

"V" squeezed and pushed her inner infection of the mind down very deep within herself to hide the real emotional truth; she felt she was now saved by the blessings of Gods inspiration in man. "V" prayed like she had never prayed before, with the entire believers firmly behind her in every sentence, "V" felt spiritually lifted and had now triumphed over immorality and the lust of the heart. "V" glorified God on high because he gave her the victory, (although in her own prayer she praised God because this minister (the Voice) had given the people a message with the inspiration of the anointing.

While closing the prayer with a self made Benediction she rehearsed so many times before and now able to ride on auto-pilot, "V" half opened her eyes and sneakily took a very good look at the young Minister God had used so wonderfully today; In doing so she began to slide back into a spiritual recession. While surveying him very carefully and closing the prayer, she caught Pastor Fischer's eye. He had spotted the loving gaze and he was curious with his eyes as if to say, "God's spirit is upon you, but how can you be looking at this man in this manner while praying in the spirit?" With this interpretation noted, "Veronica" clung to her Bible and raised her hands in the air knowing well Pastor Fischer would switch back to praising God and forget. And it worked. Hopefully!

The scene was complete. They all sat down again to eat the food that "V" had forgotten to bless and sanctify, the Christmas eve party was in full swing. While she was eating with remorse, she thought about this new and exciting young scholar who seemed to be oozing charm with no sign of easing. His

Yielding (2) Temptations

very manner for pleasantries seemed to overwhelm all the women around him. Pastor Fischer still concerned, looked at "V" with a greater intensity and bloodshot eyes. She felt ill, and her bones seemed very weak, so much so she wanted to throw up. However, although under suspicion and feeling unwell, "V" manoeuvred over to the young man to thank him for the blessed words of wisdom he gave earlier.

"V" was horrified to learn he was blessed more by her than she was by him. He bowled her over for a Spiritual Six. "V" could barely breathe, her knees were weak, the hands were sweating, and she began to pant with irregularity. She thanked him with a heated blush on her face but she didn't want him to touch her sweaty palms.

Victoria created some divine space between her and the young scholar as they talked, Pastor Fischer still lurking mischievously in the background, as if he was viewing some kind of precious investment and wasn't sure of the odds, he was talking absentmindedly to a frustrated Deacon who was having a hard time getting his important message through.

The young Scholar wasted no time; he finally asked "V" her name. "Well just call me Sister V" and he kindly asked her what the "V" stood for and She declined to tell him because she was embarrassed, he accepted warily. He formally introduced himself and said his name was Reverend Tyson Junior the 3rd but told her she could call him Reverend "T". She asked which part of America he was from? And he said "well, my father is American but I'm from the UK". Victoria found this man born and bred in Britain called Rev: Tyson Junior the 3rd very Interesting. But for now she would pursue the matter no

Yielding (2) Temptations

further, at least not while Pastor Fischer was looking.

Pastor Fischer's stares were now beyond a joke. While he was preaching or trying to preach to some new guest, his neck was straining like a overweight Pelican with a load. "V" kindly told Rev "T" the 3rd she would be happy to speak to him another time as there was something she must do right away. He stood up and gave her an embrace that changed her warped imaginary fascinational world into a reality. The embrace was so comforting and warm and ohhh, so inviting, in a funny sort of way, and the ambience of it all were too much for her to bear. She stood frozen, and then there it was; the smile that confirmed it all. He knew he had an effect on her and he knew she would have to come back for more.

The dinner ladies from the Kitchen Committee Team burst forth into the room with songs and praises as they hoisted Pastor Fischer up in their arms to the rostrum, collecting his wife along the way, "V" felt in her heart; that would keep his beady little eyes off her for a while!

The Newly appointed Minister Reverend "T" the 3rd was ushered in speed to the platform to give an address for the Host Pastor and his wife. "V"'s eyes were transfixed and embezzled by the size of his chest and broad shoulders. A hulk of a man she never had and now so desperately needed to experience in her life. Rev "T" gleamed on the platform as though it was second nature to absorb the atmosphere around him. And then the moment "V" had been waiting for, "he spoke!". With his carefully chosen vocabulary so gracefully administered with a tailored desired effect, he manoeuvred into position to give the toast to Pastor Fischer and his Wife for the hard work they had

Yielding (2) Temptations

attributed to the church for the year. The Pastor was flattered, but took his comments in caution, the Pastors mind was so focused on the innocent Sisters overloading the church with personal sexual problems, and it gave him rise for great concern.

He could visualise the spiritual headlines now, **Sisters fallen in deep lust over Rev: "T" the 3rd "Pastor turning a blind eye to fornication and high sexual activities"**. Pastor shuddered at the thought. The Pastor felt the need for immediate meditative and interventionary prayer in the heart, to dispel all forces of darkness.

Rev "T" the 3rd raised his glass in unison with the believers and wished Pastor Fischer and his wife a wonderful and prosperous Christmas and a joyous New Year. Rev "T" looked at "V" just as he was about to sip the cheap imitation Passover Wine, and smiled. He tasted it with a degree of satisfaction and pleasure in recognising "V"'s reaction and response to his flirtatious and ungodly behaviour.

With this the balloons were released and the Christian Carnival music began...

"V" went home early that night because of exhaustion, her legs were in pain, due to the accident that she had some years ago. She knelt at the bedside and began to pray, and realised the thought of listening to Rev "T" the 3rd gave her the assurance she needed so desperately in her life.

Victoria's Husband burst his way through the front door once again in high liquored Spirits. He didn't feel there was a need to wash himself before

Yielding (2) Temptations

coming to bed so she had to endure the stench for yet another long year, but she remembered the Pastors teaching on long suffering over the past year, and she thought to herself, well it has kept me thus far and her hope for change must surely be now around the corner.

Sister "V's" marriage was exceptionally challenging in the beginning of their relationship, but recently over the past couple of years it had seriously deteriorated and never seemed to improve for the better. The mental impoverishment in the stimulation of the mind and their intimate life was taking its toll. There was no unity, no love shared. Even precious moments of opportunity were never seized and capitalised. Thankfully, their two daughters, Natalie and Joy were fully grown and it meant little to them what happened sexually now. As a couple, they placed a lot of emphasis on their daughters upbringing in the early years, in giving them the care and love needed to be important thinking individuals of distinction for the 21st century.

With "V" listening to her newly found friend Rev "T" the 3rd, somehow gave her a new dimension to life, and "V" desired more, even though she understood there would be no chance in any relationship taking place, the thought was totally out of the question! But he was to her so inspiring and she thought it would be nice just to listen to his thoughts about life and his social viewpoints just one more time. "Victoria knew that her life to which she had now become accustomed and resigned to would never change, unless of course, her husband died! Everything was now in the hands of God, "V" had to trust her God with every fibre of hope she had in her. The importance of eradicating an impure and diluted mind of a selfish sexually transmitted thought must be cleansed and be removed at every opportunity.

Yielding (2) Temptations

Every time "V" had intercourse (non-spoken word in church) with her husband, she felt unhealthy and sick, absorbed into spiritual depression and a decline in her enthusiasm for worship. The ladies Ministries, led by Sister Fischer, were discussing the issue of unsaved husbands and the direct effect it had on ones own spiritual life. The Soul Ties intertwined with the unequally yoked, breaks the linkage between God and Man and leaves a strong and repugnant spiritual smell to our wonderfully fragrant inviting spirit. Frankly, any thing other than Holiness would be incompatible when engaged intimately with God. "V" felt the need to pray especially after having sex because no-one understands the real pain and uneasiness of dealing with a non-believer for many years. But she firmly believed that her change would come.

Victoria prayed hard that morning because she felt dirty and unclean. Knowing her husband could have had sex with countless other women, she became increasingly worried that she could have caught something contagious. She prayed more for sanctification and deliverance from her condition. "V" felt in her spirit that she was at the end of her spiritual tether and something quickly had to be done to rectify this situation. She needed help! Her husband has been drunk now for three days in a row, constantly shouting but never laying his hands on her physically. "V" thought she was going mad, she felt that she was never appreciated as a woman, always taken for granted with household chores and never, ever, loved like woman should truly be loved as a wife.

"V" felt like garbage at times, rubbish only fit to be put on a heap to be

Yielding (2) Temptations

ignited. With true love being absent and cast away into infinity, the petrol was applied over her unwanted love just waiting to go up in flames and transformed into ashes. With her life scattered around her like flakes of non-entity, it was as if she had no sense of worth or importance. The church was never able to help, because there was no structure in place for her to emotionally lean on and receive counselling. What would she have done in such a predicament? Could the church really have helped in this mental moment of crisis? Could the church come to the understanding that real people with real problems could be invited to come and dispose of their all in the counsellor's ears. And if this was achieved, what confidence could people have in such a counsel of councillors. Too many fractions of uncertainty had made the decisions for her without due diligence.

The Pastor was up in arms with his wife early on Sunday morning, discussing the issue on singleness and Christian morality. Sister Fischer presented a strong undulating argument in favour of the Ladies in her ministry. She firmly believed that under no circumstances, would a woman with integrity and strong Christian values, ever involved herself in fornication or adultery. Pastor Fischer was pacing and on his heels. He couldn't come clean with his true motive behind his objection, and this frustrated him all the-more. Sister Fischer seized her moment of victory in the argument and knew well the intentions of her husband's unspoken reasoning; Sister Fischer kept it quite to herself, waiting for the right moment to discuss it in the ladies counsel meeting the following week, which would ensure a maximum support when the time was needed.

"Forgetting all those things behind and pressing forward to the mark of the

Yielding (2) Temptations

higher calling" was "V"'s morning's Prayer before preparing herself for Sunday morning services.

Pastor Fischer was looking extra stunning today, with his black robe and collar and matching shoes which showed the hands of a woman's touch, namely, "Sister Fischer's", accentuated the grace and emporium of order and power of the servant of God. Pastor Fischer loved the attention to his wife's detail when being dressed. The devil was in the detail being displayed with vanity and over-eagerness, proclaiming fluency not only in speech but also clarity in the dress.

The choir was in excellent form as expected and the scripture was recited with vigour and enthusiasm. Pastor Fischer warned the Music, Worship and Choir Leaders to wear their hats and appropriate dress in preparation of the falling out of the Holy Spirit. In all the years of going to church, there never was a time when all the participating members wore their hats and suits in unison for the Christmas morning service. Pastor Fischer was in his element, untouched with human affection as he breezed into the Christmas morning Sermon. He was the Messenger of God for the hour, the moment where God would speak through his Manservant with Signs and Wonders following.

Pastor Fischer hovered over the platform like an angel holding the vials of death, facial expression of anger present with every syllable and movement of the Preacher on the platform. The congregation was stunned by the force of his words and scriptures used for illustration; it pierced the hearts and minds of the intentions already committed in the heart. Adulterous language expressed with frankness and simplicity that a 5-year-old would feel guilty for

Yielding (2) Temptations

being normal. Sister Fischer bowed her head in shame and vowed to take revenge after church.

Women and children went to the Alter under the force of the Messenger; pressure was levied on any unsuspecting member that dared not go up for more grace. It was deplorable that grown men, women and children could be subjected to such humiliation with Gods name taken in vain. This was man speaking and not God speaking. A lump was felt in everyone's throat but they dared not discuss the matter with the Messenger. Sister "V" felt ill and despondent, coming to the House of God to receive a blessing on this Lovely Christmas morning to revive her soul.

Rev "T" the 3rd was counselling two beloved brothers at the Alter, making their personal peace with God. "V", in her seat, missing out on a perfect opportunity to get close to a man she respected and was slowly becoming interested in; moved in a silent and prayerful mode, connecting her prayer request to the nearest counsellor. Sister Fischer with her motherly arms and sizeable bosom of love and authority moved the counsellor behind "V" and embraced "V" with her sizeable bosom, "V" felt trapped and disconcerted with all her attention and affection she freely gave with her whole unrestrained body.

The moment of solitude came for Sister "V" when Pastor Fischer recited the welcomed closing prayer for the service; such a relief from the uncomfortable position of two grown women in touch with each other's feeling of inadequacy.

Yielding (2) Temptations

Victoria thanked Sister Fischer for her intervention on her behalf and she hoped and prayed that God would bless Sister Fischer for the sterling effort that she had performed. She lowered her voice to Victoria's ear and whispered something to the effect of "not too long in the distant future, **your change will come!**"

After the close of service, some of the sisters in the congregation assembled in a corner. When whispers of concerned buzzed in another area of the hall, Sister Fischer went over to investigate and failed when the crowd of women dispersed when alerted to her presence.

Two hours later that evening, the younger ladies gathered in earnest at a secret meeting at the young and single Sister Strays house. The topic on the small-unwritten agenda was Pastors preaching "The Adulterous Generation" the lesson for the Christmas morning. High treason was forming in the hearts of the feminine rebellions and although they were reluctant to pursue for individual revenge or direct confrontation, they agreed on the terms and the conditions of an embargo, or to simplify it "a **Church Strike**"

The news spread like wild fire. Like a Christmas High Street rush hour without the sale. The Telephone Exchange System was busy creating revenue for the telephone companies coupled with the mobile phone networks closing the deals on the doomed Pastor Fischer. Phones buzzing at the bus stops before the rebellions got to the safety of their homely castles. It spelt rough times ahead for the Pastor Council and head of the Organisational Assembly

Yielding (2) Temptations

of GHQ. Pastor's feared nightmare had suddenly taken a turn for the worst. Spiritual-Headlines now read: **Pastor Fischer, Struggling on the Picket line to salvage Stipend salary,** Pastor couldn't sleep for the rest of the night with Sister Fischer having to take two Aspirins to handle the physical pain.

The midnight rally of gossipers networking on the exchange lines caught up with Sister "V". With the Ringleader Single Parent Sister Stray rising like the Flight of the Navigator Steering Counsel, Stray was pulling her weight of the hotly debated and contested subject of Pastor Fischer and his outrageous behaviour on Christmas morning. The thrust of her message was delivered with a quick and sharp tongue, so devastating like a double-edged-sword, designed intentionally to wound and maim the Shepherd of the flock. Sister "V" was amazed as to how powerful a sheep had become in such a short time, and her conclusion to stem the flow of mutiny was to incite the words of wisdom to her beloved Sister in whom the forces of darkness was manifesting with greater intensity. Sister "V" recited the scripture "Touch Not the Lord's Anointed" and with this, the BT line revenue was reduced by one Stray Sister terminating the call.

Sister "V" was infuriated with the prospect of the Sisters committing this Demonic driven act of defiance. It was unspeakable in the ears and minds of any decent Christian to consider speaking anything against the Messenger of God. Something must be made to eliminate and recover the damage that

Yielding (2) Temptations

Single Parent Stray was so obviously attempting to accomplish. With this thought she rummaged in her Pin-striped vanity case to recover her black book, used only in emergency to contact ministers; she considered Rev Professor Clemency, but changed her mind because of the conflict on interest with his wife. Evangelist Passover was a good contact, since he helped the Mother of Sister Alfonteen, with her immigration papers and with hands on experience delivering her Goddaughters child, he would be a loyal and reliable advocate in this situation. Sister "V" felt confident that he would be spiritually sensitive to the nature of this problem. Due to the time of the day it was not constructive for any kind of general discussion but she felt the need to disregard the hour and focus on the problem. She dialled, incorrectly dialling the number, she tried again. The phone was answered with an immediate response which traumatized Sister "V" for a moment. The unfriendly answer placed her in an insecure and uncomfortable position.

Yes what can I do for you now! "He obviously was engaged in a deep discussion of a matter that was not to his liking". She uncurled her lips and released the upper Molar with reluctance in preparation for a dialogue. Praise the Lord Evangelist! This is Sister "Victoria" Oh yes Sister "V", I'm so sorry for the rude greeting. What can I...? Is everything all right "V"? No Evangelist, No, not at all; she dispensed with the information received from the Prodigal, Single Parent, Mother of One, Stray, she began to shed tears.

Evangelist Passover coughed and fidgeted on the phone while attempting to take it all in. Sister "V" finished her explanation in minutes and paused; she waited and brushed away her tears as she expected an immediate response. He coughed and tried to clear his throat from an obstruction, the rice grain still

Yielding (2) Temptations

invading his false teeth plate caused by the premature action of answering the phone with an attitude.

The Church Strike bandwagon teams were enrolling their recruits for a direct confrontation with the Prayer Ban Group. Placards and pickets were erected with speed and efficiency, the likes never seen by a charity church organisation this century. General Single Parent Stray was seen re-arming her new devoted candidates to battle against the immoral actions of the Preacher. Investing anger and malice into every new-born babe in Christ and supplanting the seed of carnal fascism within Gods new born-again believers. The rebellion right-wing movement was now climbing towards its summit and something had to be done to bring our "Stray" Zacheus down from her tree.

The Prayer Ban Leader through the Holy Spirit was called 5 days before any signs of division were in evidence. The leader constantly in touch with God's instruction petitioned and summoned God for a divine intervention. The Lone Warrior cried out to God in the middle of the night, when visions of destructional forces of darkness encompassing the assembly were seen as an imminent sign of things to come. The Prayer Battle Cry was sounded, and the Group was on a Spiritual **Red Alert!** Spiritual veterans invaded the Alter of Intervention, with their waists tied using their notoriously famous Prayer Ban and heads covered in sackcloth in respect to God's presence, got down to business. The Lone Warrior standing alone in white with her Prayer Ban group, they tied their enlarged waists and oversized hips. With the sackcloth completely soaked in Olive Oil the excess overrunning down the well used prayer gown, she was now ready to give spiritual counsel to her waiting

Yielding (2) Temptations

prayer warriors. The veterans admired her strength and stamina in all her works of faith, hence the name branded in honour to her as Sister Chastity.

She stood under the authority of the Holy Spirit declaring war on the legions of darkness encompassing the church. Cries of mercy and deliverance were outspoken to God 4 minus days to confrontation. Hymns of victory echoed through the night while the enemies were asleep in their comfort zones. Sister Chastity was at her peak, with eager prayer enthusiast labouring through the daybreak hour, D-Day was only 3 days away.

The mission was clear and the task was humanly impossible. The Prayer group reliance on the Heavenly Father in Heaven to release and set free the forces of the evil one that had its influences on the church. Capturing and delivering the demon that was prepared for the church to take the fall for a human mistake. Could the church survive the oncoming onslaught to come, could the brethren from the Pearly-Gate church survive this attack? The Prayer Ban Group had to find the answers, 2 minus day to go.

The infamous Sister Chastity ignitioned the mercy seat for an answer. The mystery yet unravelled could not be left undone. Too much was at stake, with the young believers coming to the assembly after surrendering the souls to Christ, it was considered inconceivable for the evil-one to have his own way and deceive the young soldiers in Christ.

Evangelist Passover retrieved the rice grain implanted under the false teeth plate and was going to respond with a negative tone. Sister "V" expecting the authoritative figure of Evangelist Passover to stand up to any common

Yielding (2) Temptations

aggression to the Minister of God. She was expecting and feeling anxious for him to come forward with positive proposals. Evangelist Passover pretended that he was immeasurably tired. Forcing the need for urgent rest, he complained, saying he was not able to do anything of significance that would change the situation.

Sister "V" wouldn't have any of it and was angry with his attitude and vowed to tell Pastor Fischer about his lack of concern in this important affair. Evangelist Passover kissed his unstable teeth in defiance and said, "Well! He caused it?" Sister "V" said "what kind of Evangelist are you that you don't even worry about your own Pastor, May God forgive you" and she hung up the phone.

Evangelist Passover slammed the phone on the receiver and vowed never to answer the phone so late in the night again unless he had completed seasoning his herbs and spices for the next day's supply of ingredients for his restaurant. There was no sign of guilt or remorse for his beloved Brother Pastor Fischer while his name was being brandished and torn to shreds with lies and deceit. All he thought about was how he could muster enough publicity to have a significant effect on his bottom line profit. After all; the delivery of Sister Alfonteen Goddaughter's child had brought in a significant amount of regular customers in his new "The Last Passover" restaurant.

A powerhouse of a prayer warrior in the Brothers Mass Choir Department became alarmed at-the-now-published news of the Church-Strike. The

Yielding (2) Temptations

brothers knew his ability and strength to grab a spiritual bull by the horns and rend them defenceless. With this inner assurance given to him by the Holy Spirit, he fell on his knees and began to pray.

"He was a calm brother with a strong theological knowledge of the scriptures. A soldier with a sound mind and a strong will. His spiritual perception brimming with Solomon's wisdom earned him the right to have the name his mother so rightly recognised as being appropriate for his life, Brother Run-Tings, quite a name for a profound leader!"

Run-Tings swept the Demon Kingdom with the fervent prayer of a righteous man, clean-sweeping the legion and forces of darkness with every phrase and scripture that the Holy Spirit brought to his remembrance. Demons fled from the wrath of God, as Brother Run-Tings summoned the judgement seat for mercy and grace. Barriers erected by the forces of darkness crumbled and submitted themselves to the slavery of the cross, one prayer of a truly righteous man availed great things.

"The heavens opened up and declared the glory of God; and the firmament began to show its handy work", all this was performed, right there in the middle of the prayer. While Run-Tings laboured in prayer in the midnight hour, the Prayer Ban was climaxing to the penultimate point D-Day 1 day to go. Angels were dispatched in great numbers, cornering every part of the church, ceiling and gatepost's. All this activity was charged by the old veterans led by Sister Chastity in travail for victory in the name of Jesus!

Evangelist Passover could not sleep; he began thinking of ways to drum up

Yielding (2) Temptations

more and private enterprising business. The "Last Passover" Webb-Site was not yielding the kind of returns forecasted by the experts. Hence, with a great flash of inspiration, he got up and completely changed the approach in advertising. The message was given in a clear current conditional terms. The need for people to come "**now**" and pray for the impending Church-Strike that is due to take place any-day. The Strike was emboldened with large fonts and was enforced with emphasis. While programming Evangelist Passover smiled to himself thinking of the impact it will have on his balance sheet. The full address and name of the church was present in his advertising because the church was the official sponsor for spiritual support. He then lay back in his bed and after much mental calculation and deliberation on profit making, he fell asleep.

Sister Chastity called the Prayer Ban warriors together and with the assurance and conviction given to her by the Holy Spirit, she was convinced God would send more Prayer Warriors on the hour of battle. With this the veterans sprang to their tired worshipping feet and danced like King David did before Saul the King.

There were shouts of praises and Hallelujah's in the house as Run-Tings received the confirmation of more Prayer Warriors coming to the rescue of the saints. And with this wonderful news he hastily rose from his knees and phoned the now beleaguered Pastor Fischer.

Sister "V" still upset with Evangelist Passover took it out on her husband that very same night. He decided it was time to be sober and all lovey-dovey, crawling all over the bedroom floor in his Y-fronts and string vest, he upset

Yielding (2) Temptations

the under bed night time chamber pot of unsavoury expelled bodily fluids causing it to stain the piled carpet floor. "Sister "V" scrubbed and cleaned the foul yellow stains until only a trace of Sunlight Fairly Liquid scent was left behind. She was not amused with her husband and with this she opened her Sacred Hymns and Solo Hymnbook and quietly drifted into the spare room.

Yielding (2) Temptations

Y (2) T

Scene 2

The morning was bright and clear with a hint of snow showers beginning to fall on this festive winter's day. Pastor Fischer couldn't pray due to the undercurrent of rumours and the forecast of what was to come. Sister Fischer still heavily sedated with Aspirins, had not even turned in her sleep when she was informed of her Prodigal Sisters action against her husband Bishop Fischer.

Although Sister Fischer was not in agreement with her husband on the subject chosen for the Christmas morning sermon, Sister Fischer accepted and understood her role as the Pastors wife. Being in service for many years as a devoted wife, she learned obedience and self-control in tackling church sensitive issues with her husband. Although she was somtimes inwardly angry about difficult issues, she was forced to fast and the Pastor would often wonder why she would be singing so ceremoniously when they had a disagreement about church matters.

Sister Fischer having heard the rumours didn't feel like praying. She directly laid the blame on her accused husband for not using Solomon's wisdom and since this had severely affected her Ladies Ministry Presidency, she was in rage now tarnished with venom. Without taking medical or even her husband's advice, she took it upon herself to relieve the stress on her

Yielding (2) Temptations

Presidential and now unstable leadership campaign. This knee jerk reaction to the problem led Sister Fischer to take a few more pills to ease the stress. Her husband stood defenceless, he wanted to say something that would soothe the migraine that was developing in his wife. It was purely a reactive decision with Sister Fischer, slamming her Bible on the bedside table; she spun round to give her husband the red-eye, sending a clear unmistakable message to her supposed Chief of Command that she needed to be left alone, now!

The phone rang extra piercingly when Pastor Fischer was anxious about the current events. He managed to pray for the first time in hours, asking God for forgiveness and more grace, requesting a sign from the throne of God in confirmation of his multitude of Pre-conceived sins. He prayed with irregular honesty, he told God everything "knowing well Sister Fischer was fast asleep". His heart was now cleansed and forgiven of all his sins and he felt revived by a spirit of absolute confidence. He picked up the phone with a thunderous "Praise the Lord", re-affirming his authority in the house and his new short lived standing with God. Brother Run Tings with a high pitched excited voice of triumph, echoed through Pastors living room registering a few decibels along the way, greeting his Pastor's with Hope and Glory. "**Praise God** Pastor!". My Lord has spoken, Pastor Fischer now attentive and eagerly awaited the sign he prayed for, Run-Tings bellowed, "Reinforcement's are on the way". Pastor Fischer didn't understand the meaning; when he suddenly heard a scream coming from the once quiet bedroom of the now semi-detached ministerial couple in Christ. Pastor Fischer dropped the cordless phone on the floor and hurried like a Black Knight with a tarnished Spiritual Armour riding on an anxious wave. Sister

Yielding (2) Temptations

Fischer now staring through their semi-slit blinds so expensively fitted and positioned, glanced back at Her Bishop with bloodshot eyes. **"You see what you've, done"**, don't you **"See what you've done"**. <u>Look!</u> He approached the blinds and peeped through. Pastor's now fragile heart, filling him with fear, began to cry out to God and wept before the mercy seat spilling his all while Sister Fischer fainted.

Run-Tings still hotly connected on the line didn't understand what was happening. He deciphered that Sister Fischer with her clear and unmistakable voice said to Pastor to look at something and then repeated it louder. He then heard his Bishop crying out loud to God all by himself and with no trace of Sister Fischer voice. His spiritual sense concluded something dire had happened or was about to happen. He couldn't hang up on the line because it was live, so he paced around in his front room wondering what to do next. He suddenly remembered his mobile phone in his Omega Security uniform and he dashed to his wardrobe and got it. The last number he called was Rev Tyson the 3rd and he quickly redialled while holding on the fixed line phone.

Rev T" the 3rd was fishing in the beautiful and quiet lake of the Quays. Comforted with the effect he had on the women at the Christmas party, he felt fulfilled in satisfying his male ego. He contemplated how he was going to penetrate his impression and desires on some single and innocent victim, and remembered a well-dressed captivating woman that supped the cheap Passover Wine with him the same night.

His latest mobile phoned produced by Motorola chirped and vibrated in his breast pocket. Not many people in his private life knew his number and he

Yielding (2) Temptations

gave specific instructions only to be called in extreme circumstances. The Liquid Crystal Display flashed Run-Tings and he composed himself believing Run-Tings wanted to discuss spiritual matters again. He answered "God bless You Run-Tings Rev "T" here". Run said, "Rev.......hold on Sir something's happening". Rev "T" was patient and waited.

Run-Tings heard shouting and chanting in the distance. It seemed to him that the sound was coming from outside the Bishop's house. He then realised what was beginning to take place.

Run-Tings didn't mince his words with Rev Tyson the 3rd and told him in straight Jamaican terms, Sir, I think... NO, I charge you in the name of Jesus Sir, to come back here immediately! Rev "T" asked, why? Because Sir, the Prodigal Ladies are-at Pastors house to "Mash-Up-De-Church, Rev "T" said, what! And Run-Tings hung up.

Rev "T" was never well versed in the mother-tongue, but he knew that something was horribly wrong for Run-Tings to talk to him like that. And in haste, he responded to the call and left immediately.

The picket line drafted and enlisted by the unknown Prodigal Warrior Leader, Sister Stray, called her rebellions to order. She announced she had received a phone call from the General Head Quarters Assembly (G.H.Q), and they firmly informed her of their outrage for the ladies in the church to behave in this manor in the community. The National Bishop requested with immediate effect, for the crowd to disband and disperse. Sister Stray replied that she would convey the message, but would not accept this scandalous movement

Yielding (2) Temptations

of preacher supremacy over the ladies, any longer. Stray petitioned that a Serious "Spiritual" and "Organisational Enquiry" must happen before sunset tonight, otherwise, the media may be informed.

Rev Exodus, National Bishop from the General Assembly, summoned his secretary and the leaders from the National Office. The venue: The Purley-Gate church, Evesham. Fax's coming in from all over the country in response to The Last Passover advertisement backlogged the system of incoming filing trays. The news hit hard on the Head Office secretary's incoming e-mail-filing system when logged into the church webb-site. She scurried into the National Bishop office with the news that the story was hitting international coverage and that she was in the process of counting the many thousands of e-mail users trying to get connected.

National Bishop Exodus was in a bad mood and he vowed in his heart that he would catch the perpetrator who nationally publicised this obscene act of sorcery. Ultimately this had caused this minor problem of indiscretion to get out of hand. Bishop Exodus could not believe that the preaching on Christmas Morning Service, could end up being scandalised by a sinner within such a short time. He was now anticipating getting his spiritual and experienced hands on the culprit, and dealing harshly with the offending minister with a quick and devastating chastised blow. He loaded his car with his armed to the teeth, National Executive Ministers and his Paratroopers trailing behind in church squad vans.

Sister "V" slept in late that morning, singing all sorts of old Sacred Hymns and Solo songs for most of the night, entreating her spirit to a higher level of

Yielding (2) Temptations

praise and worship. Her spirits was freshly revived and totally misplaced the time in updating herself. She took a look at her watch in remembrance and decided it was time to go the church to pray. As she travelled through the door she held onto her Sacred Hymns and Solos Song-Book to give her spiritual uplift and strength. She meditated on God, knowing well the adversary would be prepared to meet her there.

Rev Tyson the 3rd sped through the residential area at maximum warp speed of 20mph on his manual cycle. Leaving his car behind came as a great disappointment in this hour of need. He decided in his heart he must, whatever the consequence, take his car when going fishing next time in the suburban areas in future. The cold snowflakes battered his nose as he peddled with great intensity. Sweat poured from his sweat glands and filtered through his already drenched windbreaker. Spiritually divine speed converted into raw energy, was needed to complete the rest of the journey. Carbon Dioxide seemed to surround him as he struggled to breathe. He stopped for a moment allowing his heartbeat to calm down to an acceptable level. With this moment of restoration, he prayed asking God for extra strength to finish the last leg of the way, 10 more miles and he will safely reach Old-Evesham Purley-Gates once again.

Rev Tyson the 3rd's life flashed before his eyes while resting his fleeting heart. His mother and father waving him off to school on his first day at Primaries and forgetting to give him his precious lunch box in the process. Daddy rewarded him with his own wristwatch, when he achieved first in the class for Mathematics and History.

Yielding (2) Temptations

Glancing back in the past for Rev "T" brought a smile of warmth and affection for his now deceased parents. He promised himself to visit the grave every October month in respect for the love they shared and felt in the Christian home in which he once lived.

Rev "T's" heart now relaxed and pensive, was just waiting for the adrenaline to flow at warp speed once again. The final run, breaking the final frontiers of endurance and setting the course for the Glorious home of the Purley-Gates.

Rev "T" set his cycle in position for home, with the pedals out of sync with his feet, he positioned his ankles and put hand pressure on the breaks to hold the bicycle still. The final prayer of faith resumed its course of action as he prepared to break the "cycle barrier of sound" with Gods speed. 10 more miles to the Purley-Gates and I'm home he said to himself as he began to meditate. In faith he released the breaks and held steady the handlebars and flowed with the spirit as his mind detached itself from the physical strains of the body.

Mommy is calling "Tyson" home from the backyard as he plays with his special and favourite toy, he loses all sense of gravity and time when in tune with his imaginary play-land. Mother's not included in the games when Jemima's in charge of Tyson's mind and nothing can be done to alter that. "Tyson" is king of the house when daddy is working on the buses. To "Tyson" daddy was so kind in taking the crippled people around in his proud convertible bus and not charging a penny for his services. He thought Daddy was so cool.

"Tyson" now 6 began the investigation with girls. He saw Daddy playing

Yielding (2) Temptations

with Mummy in a strange position when they thought he was in his room sleeping. Tyson heard moaning and incessant groaning as Daddy seemed to be breathing heavy. He thought he was being helpful by getting Mummy and Daddy a cool drink from the freezer to settle them for the night. He opened the door to the bedroom, milk in hand and discovered Daddy was not with Mummy but was with some-other woman. Tyson froze on the spot; not saying a word he gawked at the motion Daddy was so expertly initiating with rhythm and pace. A tear started to flow in the eyes of "Tyson Junior the 3rd" and still to this day; every-time he remembers, a tear still make itself known to the world.

(7-more miles to the Purley-Gates). "Tyson" scratched and fidgeted while trying to make sense of what was actually happening. Daddy heard weird noises coming from the lower part of the room. When he saw "Tyson" his one son crying while he committed Adultery with another woman, he flew off the bed with such speed; he exposed his lady friends private parts to the pre-adolescent world. "Tyson" thought of Mummy slaving away trying to carn tomorrows bread for the breakfast table and here he is, my Dad; doing a dirty and unforgivable act in our own home and in Mummies bed.

(4 more miles to the Purley-Gates.) Dad could never explain to "Tyson" the reason to lie to mummy about this strange woman lying in his bed. He said he was experimenting on different women or something. He promised that Someday "Tyson" would experience for himself the pleasures of having a woman and it's nothing to be ashamed of. "Tyson" remembered the look of the strange woman in Mummies bed even up to this very day. It was strange how Daddy became "Tyson's" best buddy after that event. Maybe because

Yielding (2) Temptations

Daddy wanted to make sure he didn't, under any circumstance break his promise and tells Mum his sins.

(1 more mile to the Purley-Gates.) "Tyson" believed in obedience and manners to parents throughout his early life; and although he did not have an understanding of the deceptive forces behind his father's actions, he accepted the concept of choice in women. This obviously gave rise to the many psychological imbalances in the latter stage of his life.

Sister "V" was singing praise to God in fearful anticipation of direct confrontation, she started praying intermittently to God for an extra covering of the Holy Spirit. watching the local peasants passing by from the Express City bus, weathered strong memories of catastrophes experienced in her youthful days, but she shunted these negative feelings along , and regained her focused composure on what was to come in a devastating demonic form. The Sacred Hymns and Solo's gave her a new lease of life. She sang now with increasing volume and confidence, as onlookers travelling in the same Spiritual Express frantically assessed prematurely, that medically she was mentally insane. However the Spiritual Cruise-liner surge ahead in the Spirit to the Purley-Gates now only half-a-mile away.

Bishop Exodus and his Ministerial Troops following in squad vans meant serious business, and still only a quarter of a mile to go, time was of the essence. With Pastor Fischer causing extreme damage to the Purley-Gates Church, and conspirators on every-side trying to advertise it, coupled with the "Stray" Prodigal Leader blackmailing the Church Assembly; caused the head of Bishop Exodus to wonder out of the window for a few inspirational

Yielding (2) Temptations

answers; only to find a familiar brother recently ordained by recognition from Pastor Fischer, was spotted cycling like a madman with rods and fishing tackle falling out of his bag by the wayside. Pastor Exodus realised he needed more Anointing, and began to pray for more grace to survive this holocaust.

The Purley-Gates was seized with frenzy and excitement so quickly in the morning. Evangelist Passover ordered more staff to deal with the festive rush. More patties and serviettes arrayed in size profile and disposable foods in formation in Types and style. Root-Ginger-Beer, Iron-Bru and Sorrel by the carton-load brought in to soothe the taste of the Spiritually parched. Curry-Goat, Rice and Chicken on the boil in the kitchen, with the scent rising too early for the evening diner. Evangelist Passover wanted everything to be just perfect for his sale of the century. The scene was now set for the Evangelist to make his first "Passover" killing...

The Purley-Gates echoed with the sounds of birds singing in the trees. The "Forbidden Fruit" on the church poster unstained and untouched with ungodly hands. The serenity and composed surroundings found its mark in the peasantry place of rest. Dogs kept on retractable leash's as they stretched their cumbersome legs. A distinguished quietness penetrated the eardrums of every residing resident. A calm before the storm, the tremors before the quake, the hissing before the sting of the venomous snake.

In the Purley-Gate City, scores of privately owned buses were making their unscheduled rendezvous in the parking lots and side streets. Hundreds of Prayer-Ban Christians lining the city's wailing walls. Mercy still evident in the interventionary Prayer-Ban warrior placards waving high. Believers also

Yielding (2) Temptations

came in cars to tender their support to the cause of the gospel of Jesus Christ. Coaches filed in rows of two to fit the convoys in orderly file to bring all the warriors who want to come in. Police Patrols were gathered with speed; the unexpected arrival of the Gospels-Fans brought attention to the Mayor and the town.

Sister Chastity called the Prayer-Ban warriors to order as Sister Mary-Joseph was asked to pray. The room fell silent as Gods spirit swept the room as Sister Mary-Joseph was caught up in the heavenly-realms. Prophecies were electrifying the room, as Gods people through Sister Mary-Joseph connected each one in prayer. Every-heart was linked; every-hand was touched to Gods igniting Power of the Holy Spirit that moved from God-to-man. The people were ready to move with the anointing as the stamp of approval went out to meet up with Satan and his legion.

Bishop Exodus from G.H.Q and his Trooping Ministers stepped out of the vehicles now heavily un-laddened. Fixing their Official Jackets and matching ties in accordance to Church Corporate guidelines, the troopers smelt Sunday roasts that emanated from around the street corner. Bishop Exodus was hungry, as the journey was thwarted with the unstable roads and corners, which caused his dietary requirements to put the boot in before time. Since no one was at the scene, he thought of getting a head start on breakfast. Like the President of the United State Federal Service guards the troopers opened up the pathway for the oncoming Bishop. Opening the doors of the already welcomed "Last Passover" party, the setting affected the visiting Ministers to a mouth-watering sensation. The spread was incredible; Ministerial men with wet lips dribbling on the Sweet smelling savour of Curry-Goat and rice so

Yielding (2) Temptations

early in the day. Bishop Exodus hadn't recognised the sign on the front door, so he speedily took a seat at the table. Clicking his fingers for service, a young stern looking man came running towards the leader of the distinguished gentlemen. His soles screeching on the wooden tiled floor lifted the heads of the Bishop's unarmed guards as he grounded to a halt.

Rev "T" the 3rd beleaguered in the final straight for home, was blown off course when he was surpassed by the Spiritual-Express Cruise-liners, as Sister "V" prepared herself for dismounting. In recomposing himself after the embarrassing manoeuvre of instability, he recognised Sister "V" in high Spirits of praise and worship. There was no doubt in the mind of Rev "T", that after the first glance, he was positive she saw nothing of his unprofessional conduct in panicking to stay sober-looking on the highway.

Sister "V" saw him, withered and worn, she was concerned about his appearance. Rev "T" looked bashful, but pertinent. With no sign of shame or humiliation on his expressions, he confidently held out his hand in gesture of a Christian greeting, "not his normal style of greeting, but this was the best he could do under the circumstance". Sister "V" in her heart examined the artefacts and belongings that were more than in evident disarray. The windbreaker in total dismember-ship from the hood, the fishing tackles and rods that should be evident in its little hold-all, were nowhere to be seen, the shoe on the left foot of Rev "T" was missing and distinctly visible, especially with the purley-white sock shinning through.

Sister "V" reflected on how he was so immaculately dressed in church and the first impressions he made on the ladies with his after-shave and exemplary

Yielding (2) Temptations

taste for style. Today his Likeness to some undesirable person lingering on the street in Cardboard City troubled Victoria's first impressions. Then Rev "T" spoke, and it changed everything; the debonair smile that overcame Sister "V", revealed the true authentication of the man she was beginning to love. She clasped his hand again asking what had happened to the man of God in-light of his current condition.

Rev "Tyson updated Sister "V" on Run-Tings behaviour also mentioning the important fact about the Church-Strike already taking place at Pastor Fischer house. Sister "V" wasted no time in re-grouping Rev Tyson belongings and began in haste to move towards the Parsonage.

General Prodigal Single Parent Stray seen marching on the private Parsonage lawn of the Bishop Fischer, kept to the pace when faced with the peasantry folk. She lifted her hands in authority to whip the ladies into a frenzied state of utter madness. The neighbours clearly had enough and put in calls requesting the local Law Enforcement's immediate assistance. The City Metropolitan Police clearly stretched beyond normal resources to deal with the Christian dispute. The Sergeant, making harsh decisions to call in the heavy artillery to calm the impending disturbances; even the Mayor agreed to this devastating act of aggression, just because he wanted order returned to his untarnished city. Sister "Stray" ranted and raved all the more, in full plight of armed forces breaking corners with speed and agility. The Special forces marched in unison and stood in lines conveying the un-written language of "No Entry".

The Rebellions questioned their leader, now demoted Sister Stray stood and

Yielding (2) Temptations

looked all around her surroundings and found no hiding place.

The march was on at the Wailing walls of the Purley-Gate City. Many hundred turned out in the name of Jesus to stand up against the forces of darkness. The Metropolitan Police liaising with the Leaders of each denominational assembly who turned out for the march came to an agreeable understanding that order was required. "Jesus the Deliverer" Placards were held high in joy and gladness. Knowing that victory lay ahead and God was calling in reinforcement along the way gave the crowd renewed enthusiasm. Local Church members from the Purley-Gate assemblies joined in the Songs of Praise. The placards clearly showing the message of war with Satan and his Angels gave the boost needed for more recruits to come forward.

Sister Chastity and the Prayer-Ban Veterans moved out in the Holy Spirit as God answered their prayer in a mighty and unexpected way. The Mayor summoned tanks from the Local Infantry Division. The Commander under strict orders was to begin the Military Invasion on the Christian Rebellions. Tanks and Combat Assault Vehicles of every kind streamed the street of the Purley-Gate, a movement of this size only seen in an Act of War. The Commander in Chief stopped the convoy of heavy artillery as Sister Chastity and the prayer teams looked wearily at the mass of 24 Combat assault vehicles that seemed menacingly superior to anything in its class. The Commander stepped down and held up his hand for a salute. Sister Chastity saluted back and said "Praise God Soldier". He looked puzzled but assured that it was a peaceful encounter. He motioned his orders to stabilise the unrest brewing in Parsons Corner. Sister Chastity knew by Spiritual Intelligence the cause was Satan and his Demonic Angels and requested that she and her team come

Yielding (2) Temptations

along to show him the way. The commander thought about Military Etiquette and overruled the normal rules and accepted her proposal.

With Sister Chastity and the Countries 24 Tank Infantry Division and soldiers accompanying, marching along the route to the Purley-Gate Parsonage, was quite a site.

The concrete floor began to tremble on the highway from the sound of tanks. Screams of helplessness evidently display on every face of the crowd. Police and the men in high position levied themselves on the border of insanity and panic, and then they saw the military war machines thundering down in their direction for direct confrontation. At least a thousand man strong coming in from the Wailing Wall stood still, anticipating this to be the forces of the adversary approaching. Sister Chastity stepped forward, with her party of Prayer-Delegates and the Chief Commander of the Tank Division, they negotiated together with the Metropolitan Police and Denominational Assemblies Leaders, then they were on their way forward to the Parsonage, The Purley-Gate City came alive with suspicions of some kind of Christian Military Invasion.

The Media was contacted by one of the peasantry residents, they had seen enough of this uproar created by a few Christian Extremists. Helicopters were scrambled in earnest to the scene of confrontation, as the Major-Anchorperson for the International News was briefed on the story. This was the most important story for the decade and it was to be going live on the 1 O Clock News Broadcast.

Yielding (2) Temptations

Sister Stray became defiant and ambitious with her actions. Using wit and strong language for confrontation, she began to bellow the cause again for the ladies to take up the challenge for Christian democracy. The ladies beginning to have faith in their revived little Hitler chanted and waved their Placards in unison for action. Sister Stray was relieved and uplifted when the hearts of the rebellions were not quenched with all the odds of the Law-Enforcement against them.

Sister "V" and Rev Tyson arrived at the scene of the Parsonage. Standing there in shock and amazement; they could not believe that a sheep of the flock could ever cause such uproar in a once quiet and peaceful community. They could not move! The armed police fitted with extra long truncheons had positioned themselves to barricade any on-lookers and willing participants to the violence. Sister "V" was forced to pray by the Holy Spirit for deliverance, as Rev Tyson was speechless at the masses.

Sister Fischer still passed out on her quilted cushioned sheet was unnoticed by her husband because he locked himself in the bathroom crying endlessly before God. The fervency of his prayer was so evident and felt in his dialogue with God that the dogs next door looked towards the Parsonage window to glimpse the new species that howled out through the window in extreme pain. The curious look of fascination crept in the minds of the Mongrels and Spaniels, as they passed in the lower parts of the public grounds.

Pastor Fischer had cried enough and felt it was time for decisive action, "to the surprise of all the dogs now baffled". He no longer wanted to be seen as

Yielding (2) Temptations

the Preacher who bowed out on preaching about immorality as he felt his prayer was immediately connected to God for assurance. Once again the connection he felt with God was stronger this time, without a shadow of doubt in his mind, he planned to make his wrongs right before his fellow men. For the first moments he thought of Sister Fischer and her reaction to his final decision. So he prayed some more for courage and grace to survive this intense and sensitive situation. He quickly rose from his knees, and crossed the landing to the bedroom where Sister Fischer lay. He noticed something rather strange with her breathing and position. He felt her pulse and it was fine, he was going to slap her on the face to bring her out of it and then he glimpsed the crowd once again out of the window. Police Guards with outstretched truncheons. Men in uniform dress in riot gear were ready for action as they formed outside the house. With the familiar Sister Stray rallying her two hundred strong rebellions, taunting the police with Christian placard abuse. Waves of Un-Godly messages screeched across the placard boards, initiating a response from all citizens who experienced Preacher Abuse to come and join them in this fight for Civil Christian Rights. Pastor Fischer was outraged and heartbroken, to know that these young Sisters who, almost all, were nurtured in his Nurturing Class was taught to be obedient and to conform themselves to the Word of God, without question.

National Bishop, Rev Exodus and his Executive Arm to the teeth Ministers, were in up to their teeth with Blue-Draws and sweet confectioneries. The Deputy National Secretary Rev "Sayno" with his large hunched shoulders and full-length coat, clung unto his juicy Jerk Chicken for dear life, as the peas flew off the plate with urgency in fear of consumptionism, he quietly repeated the 23rd Psalms with conviction. "Thou preparest a table before me in the

Yielding (2) Temptations

presence of mine enemies: thou anointest my head with oil; my cup runneth over," he then motioned for assistance and requested for the waiter to bring him a very large drink and more Blue-Draws.

Evangelist Passover clung unto the doorframe of the restaurant as tremors were felt from the earth. Plates filled with sandwiches expertly placed awaiting customers, vibrated around the edge of the confectionery table. Waiters anxiously waiting for more customers became suddenly afraid of forces of nature. The lampshades shifted and jerked, as the dust fell on the "Blue-Draws" and turning the colour into a different shade of grey. The numbness expressed on each Ministerial Delegate as they prayed with renewed cause. But the Bishop used Spiritual Intelligence to discover, that what was going on was actually caused by a man-made device.

Sister Chastity and her Prayer-Ban veterans paraded the Purley-Gate Church in delight and triumph when accompanied by hundreds of Prayer-Warriors and the 24th Tank Infantry Division Combat Assault Teams. It was awesome, Deputy National Secretary Sayno, ran to the door and dropped his Jerk Chicken as he gazed into the awesome power of Sister Chastity's army. All the Ministerial Delegates with confectionarys still attached to their mouths fell clumsily to the ground, "to the relief of the Insect Kingdom". National Bishop Rev Exodus, cried out in agony "**Jesus, Have Mercy**", Not recognising Sister Chastity from the old school Bible-Studies class. He rushed forward without taking notice of the placards, and begged pardon for the Minister who caused such an outrageous act of indiscretion. He pleaded with one of the Combat soldiers, and was too embarrassed to respond with empathy or regret, he consoled his leading Commander for advice and the

Yielding (2) Temptations

Commander in Chief in turn, steered his head towards sister Chastity. Rev Exodus clung to the soldier's well-shined shoes for forgiveness and mercy "it was an awful sight to be seen by his Ministerial entourage".

Rev Sayno, being the observant National Secretary, observed the placards in view for public display and realised his leader needed help in understanding the situation. He paced forward with tender ease and tapped his shoulders with a degree of uncertainty. Sister Chastity came forward in unison to re-enforce the message to be relayed but found Rev Sayno already whispering in the submissive ear of the National Bishop. Sister Chastity froze as she saw the expression on Rev Exodus's face that went from violently red and then turned adolescently purple. Sister Chastity continued forward in full grace, with a greeting in order of his now humiliated stance, she shook his hands in view of the Ministerial Party, who still was gazing at the war machines gathering for evasive action.

Helicopters were seen flying over the wires of the National Power Grid cables. The excitement in the faces of the news reporters; flew over with the live news of the Unauthorised Christian Dispute. The unexpected accompaniment of the army had given excellent front-page news headlines, as the Evening Standard re-printed its headlines in direct sequence to events.

The Commander In-Chief gave a sign for deployment to the target, as Sister Chastity resumed her seated position in the Combat Vehicle. Her Bible raised high to motion the Queens Army to press forward to the Purley Gate. The wind was securely in their sales as the armoured divisional tanks and infantry started their engines to deploy to the preliminary target.

Yielding (2) Temptations

The armed to the teeth Ministers with Rev Exodus, raced back to their parked cars, as the highway to the Purley-Gate Parsonage was crammed to the seams with followers and tanks and Prayer-Warriors with the church SWAT squad vans. For the first moment in his life Rev Exodus realised he was out-classed, out-numbered and out of ideas for a solvable solution.

The International News buzzed with a stream of excitement and unexpected impending activities. All hands now firmly on deck, they studied every move and act of military aggression against the rebellions. Half a dozen police surveillance patrols were sent out on the scene, the skies now filled with aviation patrol machines that resembled the Motion Movie; Rambo!

Sister "V" saw it was her hour of action. The skies were being filled with all different kind of helicopters. Sister Stray held up her hands in insane-defiance, determined to go the Last Mile of the way. Rev "T" confirmed it was time to move and do something immediately as the ground began to shake. A voice from a tanoy demanded the Rebellions to disband or prepare for the consequence of imprisonment. Sister Stray was not listening although some of the Rebellions tugged at the sleeve of their leader for attention, but to no avail.

Sister "V" and Rev "T" doubled backed into the park behind the garden, passing the poodle near the Parsonage. A policeman seeing them was now running at break-neck speed in pursuit, telling them both to stop, but they kept up with the pace. Rev "T" leaped over the 4 foot fence and stretched his hands to help Sister "V". Her dress was torn in the process of clearing the spiked tip

Yielding (2) Temptations

and revealed the inner thigh of a Spiritual virtuous woman. Rev "T" eyes was not focused on spiritual things but kept on running. They raced towards the back door and found it locked. Macho Rev "T" didn't hesitate and stepped back to rugby tackle the object for total submission. Sister "V" prayed in her heart for one decisive blow as Rev "T" was determined to accomplish her prayer request. He raced forward towards the back door as he remembered one pair of shoes was missing; it was too late to stop, with the momentum was already in progress, he slammed his body, seconded by his exposed white semi-covered toe and broke through with pain and agony.

Sister "V" unconcerned with the after effects called out to Pastor Fischer as she raced upstairs. Pastor Fischer still stunned by the sight of Sister Stray turned around and was relieved when he saw a familiar face. She embraced her Pastor with a tinge of compassion, while Rev "T" followed with a limp and looked and observed with a frown. Rev "T" acknowledgement was a nod to indicate his presence. Rev "T" requested to see Sister Fischer, Pastor remembering her strange conditioned when he saw her last, raced into the other room.

Sister Chastity with her Prayer-Ban Veterans and the 24th Tank Infantry Division, coupled with Combat Assault Squad and the Christian Army from different Denominational Assemblies around the country, and with Jesus by her side was elated with God's divine movement, working in mysterious-ways.

Sister Stray and her Fascist compatriots lifted their hands in total defeat when faced with the awesome Power of God through man. The mighty forces of

Yielding (2) Temptations

God, translated into war machines against the forces of darkness were too much for the devil and his compatriots to take. They laid down the placards and faced the music of Prodigal Shame. In the heat of the moment; the heart of Sister Stray collapsed with a sudden stroke and fell to the floor, to her rebellion's consternation. A woman in black seen running to her aid sat beside her as she administered some kind of smelling salt in a cloth to the nose. Within seconds Sister "Strays's" arms fell violently to the ground and the Medics rushed in from the Military Personnel to continue the treatment required. The strange woman dodged through the crowd, and disappeared as silently as she had come. .

Pastor Fischer gave Sister Fischer two hefty blows to the cheek, as Rev "T" thought his actions were too aggressive for a positive and immediate result, he shifted his position to a more controlling stance and then lifted her head for a closer observation. And noticed her Pupillar were not positioned in the correct place and diagnosed she needed immediate assistance from the Ambulance Service. Sister "V" set out for the downstairs living room and dialled 999 for immediate medical assistance. The operator, "seeing the commotion on Cable TV" instructed her just to walk outside, as she could guarantee some medical officers were standing by helping the Ring Leader Prodigal Stray to recovery.

Sister "V" wasted no time. She bellowed out to Rev "T" to bring Sister Fischer downstairs unto the front lawn. Rev "T" needed no more information to carry out her instruction, he moved out in limping confidence as Pastor Fischer trying to hold back Rev Tyson "in fear of the outside drama", held unto his arm and almost tipping Rev Tyson and his good lady over. Rev Tyson shoved the condemned preacher to his bedside corner as he focused on taking

Yielding (2) Temptations

one limping step at a time, as he travelled down the stairs with his still fragile and painful toe.

Pastor Fischer reached a point of no-return. The floor vibrating with re-enforcement from the superior power of the aggressor and the pulsating voice of surrender from the wide-angled speakers on board the police patrol helicopters, and remembering what Run-Ting informed him about re-enforcement were on the way, with excitement; sent Pastor Fischer into a Preachers-Post-Mental-Depression.

Yielding (2) Temptations

Y (2) T

Scene 3

Run-Tings continued in his prayers of faith that same afternoon. Receiving the victory was his main concern. The immense presence of the Media helicopters and Police Patrol Machines, invading the newly up-and-coming church of the Purley-Gates gave rise to some serious concerns. He turned on the television to update himself on the current situation.

The Anchorperson initiated the outline of the dire-situation on the loss of life experienced at the once quiet and peaceful area of the Purley-Gate. Brother Run-Tings clung to his Bible with disbelief, and could not believe the evidence when it was shown on National TV. The volume of Military traffic shocked Run-Tings, his heart brought on irregular heat-waves by just seeing it in living colour. Military Personnel carried three stretchers outside of what looked like a Preliminary Militarised zone. With Gospel-Fans silent in respect for what seemed to be survivors from the struggle for Christian Civil Right Fascist Movement gone horribly wrong. The Anchorperson interrupted the picture to bring an announcement from the Chief Minister of Defence, (Downing Street).

The National Emblems for the commonwealth were displayed with honour and glory. The pride of Britain's anthem rendered in the background was swelled in the ears of the listeners as they followed on. The Minister of Defence; Sir Ronald Cato, presented his hermeneutic explanation of the

Yielding (2) Temptations

serious situation that had developed. He apologised profusely for the outrageous action in this circumstance and vowed to initiate a full and joint Military and Metropolitan Police enquiry with immediate effect. Sir Cato gave his word of honour as a soldier and promised that there would be no stone left un-turned until the truth was revealed. Coming to the climax of his oratory speech, he indicated with a heartfelt sigh, his personal and emotional feeling of regret that such a miscalculation of events could have caused this tragedy to happen. The Anchorperson rumbled back into the picture prematurely. With files and ill-prepared sheets scattered around the desk so evidently before the viewers, she scrambled into a intellectual recap mode without a cue.

Run-Tings closed his eyes to review the bullet points of these events in his mind. He looked to God for answers, but found none. The stillness of the afternoon sun begun to rise with a taste of sorrow and ill-conceived pain; the vibrancy he experienced in the early days was gone and never to be returned. The loss of life was too much to bear and he demanded that God give him the full spiritual explanation to this conundrum of activities.

Sister "V" and Rev Tyson sat together in the City-Gate hospital in after shock from recent events. Sister Fischer was admitted for mental examination and a thorough analysis was undertaken to explain the bruises on the face. The doctors had to consider wife battery from physical violence; hence, the Psychologist was flown in from one of the top specialist centres in the country. The Military spared no expense to get their very best Psycho-Physician on the job.

Yielding (2) Temptations

Reluctant Professor Meseh Callme, Phd,MD, had another agenda on his mind. He was following the foul-ups demonstrated by the Ministry of Defence and concluded, although un-researched, his findings were viable for a head-to-head confrontation with the army. He believed with an inner-conviction that the time had now come to take vengeance with full exposure to the media. With a smile he hung up the phone on the Chief of Military Defence as he accepted the offer to investigate this Military blunder.

Professor Callme, saw his chance. The treatment rendered to him by his cruel and evil father "General Callme" who had whipped his hide for not studying hard enough to get good grades at the Grammar School Academy. The Professor came second in his class and still his father didn't recognise his intellectual ability in him. His father could only see, "The Queen and Country" and nothing else mattered in his mind for his son's future. The Professor cried tears of psychological pain; day and night he was forced to study even harder to compensate for his impaired vision prescribed by the Optician. His Father was furious and blamed his Mother for not feeding him with the right vegetables that now caused his eyes to be less than 20-20.

Professor travelled to the blunderous scene with strong intentions to support the Christian movement and to damn the Military act of aggression with full media support.

The crowd was distilled and focused, while the news of the victims of the dispute was carried away. The once joyful town now turned into sorrow, the pain filtering through every genuine believer of Christ. The unknown woman in the distance lit a candle in respect for the dead, as the prayer for clemency

Yielding (2) Temptations

were levied on the shoulders of the guilty. Nightfall was approaching as the tanks and soldiers sent out in error, began to leave in a sombre mood. The soldiers promised to come back to the church as a mark of respect to the deceased. In their hearts they felt responsible for the heavy actions implemented on the Good Citizens of the Purley-Gate and asked forgiveness for their involvement. Regretfully the response was not forthcoming and after returning to the Barracks, they left the army vehicles and returned after changing into their full complimentary honoured uniforms, as a mark of respect to the now "Confirmed" dead.

The news was at fever pitch. Every reporter in the land wanted to bite his or her journalistic teeth into some action. The CNN News pilfering on the outskirts; trying to extract vital pieces of information for worldwide News. Anchormen and Women all around the world were primed with updates of the current situation. Editors scrambling to re-address the front page of their respective newspapers became mandatory. It was an Editors dream, millions of copies would be sold at the expense of a death, and another tragedy was beginning to emerge from yet another indiscretion. It now became a worldwide scandal.

THE HEADLINES NOW READS:

THE MIGHT OF THE BRITISH MILITARY, MOVE IN TO DEAL WITH THE CHRISTMAS SERMON FROM THE LOCAL PASTOR "FISCHER"

Yielding (2) Temptations

Sister Chastity felt like a failure, although a victor, her heart sank to a new all-time low. She motioned her beloved new-found brethren to head back to God's house for a vigil. Unanimously, everyone agreed by the nodding of their heads. Three thousand souls marched through the streets of the Purley-Gate City to pray and comfort each other at God's house. With the news helicopters monitoring the procession, they knew within their hearts, the impact it would have on all believers all over the country.

The Soldiers were already there, five hundred strong in uniforms, each holding a lit candle. The street was cordoned off with blockades. Police and Ambulance vehicles parked idly by waiting for the unknown to happen. Tears of compassion flowed down many faces when a talented singer rose up to sing "Amazing Grace", on the makeshift platform. Every Atheist mind was quashed with the perfect pitch of her voice; every hardened heart was filled with genuine compassion; unbelievers began to think again about his/her Salvation. As she sung her second rendition, "Blessed Assurance, Jesus is Mine..." Candles arrived by the van load and were distributed to every person on the street. Runners with lighters appeared out of nowhere, igniting the candles for the all night vigil partakers, it was time for the all night marathon vigils to begin.

The now shameful National Bishop, Rev Exodus, and his Un-Armed Ministerial Party from G.H.Q took a back seat from current events. Rev Exodus still outraged with the news going to the media without prior warning, gave him ammunition to seek the culprit concerned. He commenced his investigation with immediate effect. His Ministerial party of high moral standards were dispatched like pizza couriers to survey the area and report

Yielding (2) Temptations

back with their findings. Their mission; **Find the Grasser!**

The "10 O Clock News" interrupted the scheduled programme for the evening. An anxious reporter outside Purley-Gate hospital read from his carefully worded statement. The news that he was about to expose to the world would change the entire course of events. He proclaimed in full view of the camera, "This evening, ladies and gentlemen, we have come to you with a grave report. The Ring-Leader known as "Sister Stray" was murdered at the Purley-Gate site this afternoon. The test has been returned conclusive, that she was "Murdered" with Chloroform applied to the nose approximately 4-5 hours ago. Anymore new developments will be relayed in the 11 O Clock News." The camera's focused on the scene of the crime with a deafening silence.

Rev "T" fell on his knees with the news of the murder. Sister "V" comforted the young Minister with genuine heartfelt affection. She placed her Sacred Hymns and Solo's book on the Cafeteria table and began to sing with tears in her eyes and sadness in her heart. "Draw me nearer, nearer, nearer blessed Lord, to the cross where thou hast died.....". The words dissolved into infinity as did the tears, she was overcome with emotion. Rev "T" and Sister "V" sat arm in arm crying over the murdered Young Sister, Mother of one and now deceased "Stray".

Pastor Fischer concealed in his private room under Military guard; in fear of reprisals, turned over in his sleep from the sedatives prescribed by the doctor. They found him in the Parsonage bedroom chanting and squealing like a little girl out of control and felt it necessary for the Medical Personnel to strap him

Yielding (2) Temptations

to a stretcher, preparing him to be dispatched to the nearest Observation Ward. The doctors weren't happy with his slow progress. They expected him to have snapped out of this Semi-Depressant State a long time-ago. Pastor concealing his awareness of the activities around him, feigned his illness to buy-time for a period. Pastor could not handle the intricacies of a murder investigation, but vowed in his heart to keep the lie going for as long as he could. He knew within himself that there were inconsistencies that some day would be exposed. The secrets beyond the eyes-and-ears of the church would be devastating to his already tarnished reputation, if found guilty.

The cold-blooded murderer kept running in the midnight mist, through the trees, into the valleys and passing through the hedges, and ending in the cooling place of the garden shed. She placed her worn garments into a black (self-sealing bag and disposed of it in the garden hedge-burner drum. The trainers now soiled with mud were placed with the garment for incineration). A thorough and complete job was to be implemented for no incrimination. She felt safe after taking off her wig. After speaking to Pastor Fischer in his moment of greatest need earlier that morning, she was enraged at the behaviour of Sister Stray's actions. The woman in black must protect her man, although a Preacher and married to a devoted wife, she still felt he needed protecting. The groaning she experienced while talking to Pastor drove her to this insane act of pre-meditated murder in the first degree. It was her moment of truth, she loved him with all her heart, and nothing in Heaven or in Earth could stop it's manifestation through her actions of love. If anyone, coughed, sneezed or even touches her man in any way unseemly, they would pay for their unauthorised actions with the ultimate cost. Taking careful note of the time, she decided to go back to the all night vigil as herself.

Yielding (2) Temptations

The candles were lit by thousands of people entering the hour of prayer. The focal point for the early morning's sacrifice was for the deliverance of Sister Fischer. No change was mentioned by the reporters as they televised the update in open-air. The people were not concerning themselves with the condition of Pastor Fischer, because they left the verdict to the mercy of the General Assembly, Military and Police

General Exodus crouching beneath the church Stairs was in a direct mobile communication with the National Church Secretary. She briefed her leader on the development on the Passover Internet response and suggested that the Ministers should check out the place for clues on, **who done it!** Rev Exodus agreed.

The first wave of the ministerial pizza courier information service team returned within minutes of being sent out. Rev Exodus finished eating his sandwich salvaged from the Passover Restaurant and shuffled closer to hear the good news. Minister Judas king stepped hastily forward with results. "Reverend, didn't you say at the Head Office that there was a Webb-Site in the name of The Last Passover?" Rev Exodus nodded in agreement. "Well Boss, the very same place we had breakfast this morning (bowing in shame) is the very place, called; The Passover Restaurant. With the crumbs still visible from the salvaged sandwich remains in the hands of the National Bishop, he brushes all the remaining evidence from his palms and clenched his fist in heated anger. The other pizza parties arrived back to the rendezvous point with no new news but they listened to the new revelation with shameful interest.

Yielding (2) Temptations

The midnight vigil was a Godsend. Evangelist Passover couldn't believe his luck. Hundreds of people answering to the request of his beck and bottom-line profit-increasing call. The food disappeared so quickly; his reserves stocks were emptied from the fridge before he could finish cooking them. The staff worked around the clock. Earning their overtime rate-of-pay of time and a half; gave the waiters an extra spring in their step, this was to continue for an unlimited period. Evangelist Passover strutted across his forecourt, with his hands firmly behind his back, and tilted forward on his toes with glee. The sensation sent waves of monetary emotions, as he mentally counted his profit ratio. He felt safe, no element of risk, and only a good hard earned, well thought out, business plan that now had been so profoundly proven to be a reality.

Dressed in a black-cape, black suit, and matching shoes, complimented with his brightly coloured professional bow tie, Professor Callme arrived at the church with one of the Ministry of Defence Advisors. The Professor looked sharp, and the National Bishop looked puzzled as to who this was. The Professor noticed their curiosity and drifted forward towards them (with his cape rising in the midnight breeze). Professor thrust out his hand in unison with a greeting; I am Professor Meseh Callme, sent from the Ministry of Defence.

Grown seasoned Ministers from the National Assembly disgraced their Leader Rev Exodus by crouching and holding (firmly without success,) their rumbling belly laughs, with spits and spurts of uncontrollable saliva spewing all over the stairs of the sanctified building, created quite a scene for the Bishop. He thumped his feet on the ground to achieve order, but to no success.

Yielding (2) Temptations

When he had enough of the shame, he sent them again on another pizza run for peace and quiet. The National Bishop had to come clean with the Professor, and he informed him of the reason for his delegate's behaviour. His very unusual and unique Name. The professor just shrugged his shoulders and asked if there was a place where they could have a quiet chat. The Bishop unfamiliar with the setting, requested that one of the Stewards open the church office, so they would be allowed a little privacy.

Sister "V" and Rev Tyson still waiting at the hospital, were not told of any changes and felt useless sitting and waiting for something to happen. Rev "T" decided it was time for them to leave, but first he went to tell the receptionist to call their numbers if there was any change. And so, in the very early hours of the morning, as the snowflakes began to fall; they left the hospital. That night had been cold and blustery and the full moon still shone through the overhead branches onto the pathway, giving a comforting feeling as Rev "T" held Sister "V's" quivering body. She was responsive to his warmth. The feeling of a real loving and affectionate man, touching a sensitive feminine body, created a connective bonding that would soon turn into a weave. Rev Tyson" still wasn't satisfied; she was still cold. He unclenched her waist as he unzipped his windbreaker to wrap around her shoulders, and said "Now isn't that better?" she nodded with a chilled approval. The walk was long, and with no Public Transport at their service, it was going to be a long walk home. Rev "T" thought about the journey and realised that his home was much nearer than hers, so it would be logical for them to go back to his place, because she lived at least 4 miles further away. He hesitated to mention straight away the singularly decided proposal, thinking that she would reject his taking the initiative straightaway. As he got closer to his own homely destination, his

Yielding (2) Temptations

conscience got the better of him, and he just came out with it much louder that he had intended. "Do you realise "Sis" it's late and its cold? And since I live closer to our present position, don't you think.....?" Victoria pre-empted his thoughts and cut him off. "No Sir. I certainly do not think it....! (She glared at him). "I'm sorry, I'll walk you home all the way then, please forgive me?" Sister "V" now quickened the pace. (In her mind she thought) She hardly knew the man, and here he was, asking her these unthinkable things! Who does he think he is? Coming on to her this strong without even kissing her first!..Oops! What was she thinking; this is all wrong, "Just get me **Home, Now**!" She exclaimed; she raced ahead with her Sacred Hymn and Solo Hymn Book swinging more vehemently along the path.

The National Bishop and Professor Callme warmed to each other when they discussed their preliminary objectives. The professor agreed with the Bishop on catching the culprit responsible for delivering this indiscretional situation caused by Rev Fischer to the Media. Their plan was to ultimately crush any blame levied on the General Assembly and totally cripple any organisation that supported this scheme. They shook hands as they began to formulate their detailed plan for immediate action.

The Professor felt he was beginning to make progress. His newly appointed Ministerial scouts were working for him now, which gave him an advantage for more eyes and ears on the ground. The second phase was to begin, to establish who murdered the Rebellious Leader. He needed some local intelligence that could provide some answers to his shopping-list of questions.

The National Bishop briefed his Spirit filled Ministers on the new plan of

Yielding (2) Temptations

action. The Ministers were excited and eager to put on their dark Ministerial shades. With Rev Exodus reminding them of their unacceptable behaviour with the name Professor Meseh Callme, and gave them a stern warning of the operation at hand. Due diligence and wisdom was called for. And he expected every Minister to fulfil his role in delivering results.

Evangelist Passover couldn't have enjoyed himself more. The extra overnight supplies, reamed in like clockwork, right on time. Pound Signs very evident in his eyes as the delivery of Patties and Rundowns were placed into the selling position for maximum exposure. More men in suits came tumbling through the door for seconds, (Passover thought), but most of them were more interested in the building and the style of architecture, than having a genuine desire for food. Evangelist Passover thought for a moment, and reviewed in his mind the risk with the Inland Revenue Inspectors making an appearance. He frantically shoved more confectionery their way and tried to be friendly, only to be told that they were not interested in what he had to offer, that they were there to examine the efficiency of the business. This brought a chill down the Rundown spine of Evangelist Passover. Ministerial Delegate Joshua King, smiled to himself when he got Evangelist Passover on the ropes.

Sister "V" finally reached home in a very bad mood. She didn't talk to Rev "T" for most of the way and he was too embarrassed to care about the small matter of dialogue. Unleashing her fury at his suggestion of a stopover, she slammed her front door in anger, and without wilfully intending to, the door made contact with his nose. He painfully retreated to her gate for a safe distance. She glanced through her moonlit curtain to survey the un-repairable damage to the Rev's nose, but he walked off down the path with his head

Yielding (2) Temptations

throbbing with nasal pain. She thought about her actions, and felt bad. Her Husband climbed down the stairs and called out "V" is that you?" yes honey, it's me! "I take it you had a rough day ehh?" Can we talk about this later? I have to get some sleep. Her husband moved aside to let her pass to go to the upstairs landing and through to the bathroom.

Rev "T" had had enough, his nose, his toe and now his pride was hurt; all in one day, surely nothing worse could happen.

The vigil continued through the night with Redemption songs and hymns brought in by the Old-Timers. Sister Chastity and her Veterans sang the night-away with Gods divine blessings and grace, they began to testify of the victory through Jesus, as it warmed the hearts of the believers present. The killer was sitting with her candle and was laughing with others while warming herself with the midnight burner. She fitted in just fine in the crowd of the genuine Christians. Sister Chastity suddenly became challenged and alarmed when the Spirit of God revealed the presence of an Evil-Spirit at the Early-Hour-Vigil. She spoke in an unknown tongue as the Spirit gave her utterance. The Spiritual Veterans moved into action, as they began to encircle the territory of the church mass. People were seen moving around as the Lord began to speak to several individuals all at the same time in unknown tongues confirming his word The killer got up, and mimicked others as they moved around in two's and threes. Instead of the killer encircling the mass like the others, she disappeared behind a tree and headed for the woods. Two thousand people were seated on the grounds when God moved and only a few people saw the killer leave the site in a hasty fashion. God spoke and the Devil ran, and within moments of the killer leaving the camp, peace returned to the

Yielding (2) Temptations

Christian Body of Believers.

Pastor Fischer still pretending woke up from his sleep. He found himself surrounded by men in dark-suits and stethoscopes. They were discussing his condition. They glanced at him when the pitch of his snoring level changed, due to his now conscious state; he had to find a new acceptable level to convince them he was only perturbed by their conversation. He fidgeted and frowned and gradually raised the snoring level back to a convincing tone; it worked! They continued the conversation. The Consultant indicated his professional findings. He was adamant, that this patient was in a fine condition and that nothing was wrong with him. Pastor Fischer tensed, (as he was unsure what was going to happen next. Maybe they would run some reflex tests on him with large wooden mallets, or reflex tools to test his nerve reactions). The Consultant ordered them to take him to The Military Hospital for them to have a closer observation. The accompanying Doctor filled out the papers for Pastor Fischer to be released to the Military Hospital.

Pastor Fischer knew he was in deep water, especially now it was a murder case. He began to pray, but it was too late. He had reached another point of no return and this time it was the military that were in charge. They carried his bed through the halls of the newly sterilised section and squeezed it into an elevator heading for the basement. Pastor Fischer could smell the Menthol as he passed the secret laboratories. The scent of death wafted over him as they passed the morgue. Pastor dared not open his eyes to observe where they were taking him, and then the outside air hit him hard with a chilling blow. They lifted Pastor onto another stretcher but this time, it was less comfortable. It was hard and leathery. A smell not usually associated with hospital

Yielding (2) Temptations

equipment, and it terrified the Pastor. He wanted to get out of his pretence sleep, but he couldn't. He didn't have the nerve to look, when he was being transported. Pastor felt doomed, and deserted. No Brother, no Sister, no Wife to help him in his hour of desperate need. Pastor repeated the 23rd Psalms, "Though I walk through the valley of the shadow of death, I will fear no evil," he could not bring himself to say "for thou art with me......" because he was there and because he was guilty, guilty as a common sinner.

Run-Tings praying through the night, woke up Rev "T" very early in the morning, and Rev "T" who was still tired after the long walk home, hesitated to answer his phone. Run-Tings wanted an update on the current situation, but Rev "T" was reluctant to get into any debate at this early hour of the day. Run-Tings detected fatigue and tiredness, and wanted to say something that would arouse his attention. **Run-Tings swallowed hard to give Rev "Tyson" another Spiritual Inspirational Blow. Rev**? **God spoke to me last night about Pastor you-know!** " Ah Ha" **I said, the Lord spoke to me last night about Pastor Me-seh!** "What did the Lord say Run-Tings?" **Sir, are you ready for this?** "Come on Run-Tings just spit-it-out man!" **The Lard told me that Pastor Fischer is having an affair with a dangerous woman!** "Say What!" "What did you say Run-Tings," (as Rev "T" flashed the bed-sheet from off his bed) Run-Tings took charge and delivered the message from the Throne-of-God. Rev "T" couldn't believe it. Run-Tings had never been known to be wrong, but with this revelation, un-substantiated, would cause all sorts of problems, with all the National Assembly and Ministerial Parties all present. It would make it impossible for Pastor Fischer to get even a fair trial. Run-Tings! Don't be hasty now. Let's take this one step at a time. Rev "T" had to convince Run-Tings to hold on to the revelation until proof was found,

Yielding (2) Temptations

before anything was to be said to anybody. Run-Tings reluctantly agreed.

Rev "T" hung up the phone and paced around in his boxer shorts on the landing, thinking on what to do next. He was in a spin, completely mesmerised by the sequence of events, he needed help. Sister "V" came into his thoughts but he remembered what had happened a few hours ago. He didn't care, all he thought about was to share this big problem that weighted down his young tender Pastoral shoulders. He had no time to waste; he had to move fast. Shoes; where are my shoes, he said to himself, car keys; where did I put my car keys. Fumbling through all of his previous trouser pockets, he found the keys he was looking for. Teeth; must brush my teeth. After giving a few anxious moment of attention to hygiene, he left the house in speed to Sister "V's" marital apartment.

Sister Chastity was advised by her colleagues to take a rest for a couple of nights from the all-night vigil. Tired and still full of life, sister Chastity reluctantly obeyed their commands. They moved in another heavyweight prayer champion. One that could cause serious ripples in the impending investigation, a person that could so easily sabotage the efforts of the Military and Metropolitan Police with one revelation. It was time to turn up the heat on the culprit, and cause mayhem to the guilty offender. Run-Tings was summoned to the Vigil with an escort to further him on his way.

Yielding (2) Temptations

Y (2) T

Scene 4

The birds in ariel view were looking on the Purley-Gates in curiosity as they sang their morning tunes. The vigil audience in radiant praise and worship to God admired and followed the melodies of nature. Thousands of small insects gazing in wonder at the activity above their little worlds, people stampeding on the ant mounds caused shock waves to the underworld kingdom, as they prepared themselves for imminent battle of aggressive war. Legions of foot soldier ants went to their queen for help, arguing the motion and action plan for continual survival. The Bull Terriers looked on in wonder, as they seemed to be the centre of attention. They lifted their little muzzled heads with pride as they strutted forward in vibrancy and stubbed tails waggling high. The felines hiding behind the fences were cautious as many hands tried to stroke them with unsuccessful attempts. Fox and Hounds were kept at bay due to the sheer numbers of bodies that could cause stress and ultimately pain. The protection of the animal civilisation was at stake, and every step had to be taken to protect its existence.

The people marching on in worship stretched their tired legs as they laboured through the night with renewed enthusiasm. Run-Tings was summoned up to the camp to run things as Sister Chastity took a well-earned break. The people eager for another phase of worship, waited in patience as they were led in

Yielding (2) Temptations

songs of praise. The Gospel worship leaders sang to the Lord to bring the crowd to another level of praise. Run-Tings was going to make a difference. It was time for a real intercessionary session. And it was time to cry out to God in fervency for answers.

Sister "V", in her single room bolted through her bedroom door, as burglars; it seemed, tried to break down her front door. Her husband already alert to the break-in attempt was ready for action with his baseball bat in hand. Sister "V" in her night-gown and her husband in Y-fronts and no other covering approached the door with heavy breathing. Rev "T" was not going to be perturbed, he was adamant. He knocked on the door with a renewed ferocity. Sister "V" cried out in anger, as her husband raised his bat. "Who is it?" Rev "T" paused as he saw her reflected shadow in the frosted moulded glass. Open the door at once! I need to speak to you right away. It's important sister V! Her husband now furious that a dialogue was being initiated without consent; He, the man of the house, released the door-catch and raised the weapon in self-defence. Rev "T" was forced forward with a sudden unexpected blow to the side of the head. The lights went out for Rev "T" as he clung on for dear life to the shoulders of her husband. He shrugged his shoulders in delayed regret, as he turned his back on the injured victim. Sister "V" cried out "Oh God! Have mercy" as she fell to her knees and lifted the young Ministers head with tender loving hands. Her husband glanced back at "V" for sympathy, only to find her cradling the young minister within her unrestrained bosom. "V" cradled him in her bare arms and soothed him in the midnight hour, scent of bodyoils surrounded his tender throbbing head. With a gentle wave of her hand across his forehead, Rev "T" came back around to his senses with a smile. The husband placed the lethal weapon on the floor, as he was itching

Yielding (2) Temptations

for "V" to relieve him from his sins. Rev "T" still paternally attached to Sister "V", staggered with her towards the kitchen table for support. He looked around the kitchen as the animated birds flew around his Christian Halo. Focusing on an object nailed to the kitchen wall brought a new sense of uneasiness. Knives were professionally arrayed in neat rows for the expert butcher. The cleaver conveniently placed in order for the efficient executionist, the blood-stains still evident on the chopping board from the innocent lamb that he had prepared for Sunday diner, and the smell of death that emanated from the kitchen dustbin, that Sister "V" had begged her husband for days to empty. The husband truly was a killer and Rev "T" felt helpless to defend his rights as a Minister. Rev "T" felt battered and beaten to a pulp, and it was without provocation and he was angry that an honest innocent person could be subject to such physical brutality. Sister "V" sat beside him while the husband felt sick but unrepentant, he finally went to his room in a fury, as he took one more glance at the intruder along the way. Sister "V" looked again at her Minister and a new seedling feeling of passion began to emerge from nowhere.

Their eyes connected; their moistened open lips only inches apart, the wondering fingers touched the tips of nerve endings, shattering all the feelings of the innocents brought about a new phase only experienced when a new birth of affection emerges with a new vitality. The world stopped, the cold sweat burrowed through the sweat glands and made themselves recognized to the known world. The excitement, the claustrophobia in open air encapsulated the moment never to be forgotten. It was time for "Love", but she remembered her position in life, and "FEARING GOD" was more important.

Yielding (2) Temptations

Rev "T" cleared his passion-infested throat, as he looked into the now refocused eyes of Sister "V" as he managed to remember with great difficulty his purpose for coming. By standing up in her kitchen with all the evidence of butcherism, he came to his point, as Sister "V" absorbed with great difficulty, Rev raced through the information that Run-Tings had imparted on the phone.

The room was cold and mouldy, with a hint of sweaty armpits lingering through the air of the already cluttered room. With pencils and papers streamed across the mahogany desk for note taking, It was time for the dreaded interrogation to begin. Not so comfortable as in his previous hospital surroundings, he found himself strapped to a chair and half gagged with sealing tape to prevent him talking to any unauthorised Agent from the Military Base. It was confession time for Pastor Fischer, no escape; no help from the outside world could save him now from the onslaught to come. He thought of ways to hold his peace, keeping his unruly tongue under strict subjection. His time was short and he had to think of ways to quickly strengthen the odds of his hidden secrets being found out. He prayed with increasing urgency, asking God for divine guidance in his premeditated sin. He received no confirmation from Heaven that his prayer was reaching anywhere, now he knew he was beyond "Saving Grace" and he could not bring himself to ask God for forgiveness. Then suddenly the lights went out for the night. He screamed and shouted in fear of evil Agent's reprisals. The night chill coursed through his veins in conjunction with his fear of the unknown. The full moon illuminated the night sky as the mist floated past the trees; it was going to be a long night. "His weeping will endure for the night" but no "joy was coming in the morning" he fidgeted and yelled as a rat touched his ankles in hot pursuit for food. Pastor Fischer realised he has just

Yielding (2) Temptations

arrived in the Military Hell and he started to feel the midnight heat in the moonlit night.

Evangelist Passover bowled-over with Judas Kings comments, was sent on a phantom goose-chase. He hurriedly thrashed out all of his receipts on the office desk to assemble and sort out into some sort of chronological order. Judas King was so pleased with his performance and strategy, he presented the new information to his leader, Bishop Exodus, giving his additional input to the master plan, which was created by Professor Callme and the National Overseer, Bishop Exodus. The Bishop nodded with a sign of approval as he waved him off to continue his pre-planned schedule of investigations.

Professor Me-seh Callme studied Pastor Fischer with curious eyes. Focusing on the Physicians notes on the condition of his former patient, he knew that Pastor Fischer was playing games and the Professor was determined to crack him, even if it would be the last thing that he would accomplish. His intention was not to incriminate Pastor Fischer but just to get him talking. All the Professor wanted was enough information to catch the killer and to expose the Military to the media. The professors eyebrows lowered and raised with every new and interesting thought. The logical process of interrogation will be long and gruesome, and with his first civilian as a suspect informer, he had to tread very carefully with the information received. The Professor cooled Pastor Fischer off for the night to force him to his senses, he heard the screams, the Professor had planted the hungry rat, and he heard him pray out loud to heaven for deliverance. He was not unconscious after all! And the doctors were right!

Yielding (2) Temptations

Pastor Fischer struggled through the night in torture and torment. The evil spirits that surrounded him in rodent form weakened his psychological defences. In pursuing his pre-meditated innocence, he thought of self-levitation of the mind and spirit to the transitional world, (a book he read some months ago). Now determined to grasp his newly informed knowledge, he set out to deceive everyone with a convincing performance. Levitating the mind? He thought, how could he levitate his mind? A bulb illuminated in his head, spurred on a new surge of inspirational current as it was translated into an idea. He knew what to do. The body had to be reformed to his new strategical plan. Pastor Fischer was now confident that he was ready for any test or interrogation they had planned for him. The morning came with New Hope for Pastor Fischer. Now confident he had all the answers, he began to Levitate into his transitional world.

Run-Tings gathered the people together in prayer and worship as he dramatically rode the prayer warriors to another level. He stood tall on the Preachers soapbox and declared to the people the agenda for the day's session. He announced with conviction the need for the people to cry out to God in supplication and mourning, for the interpretation of the current events now in progress. He orated the need for the people to listen to God's voice for the revelation, and act according to the leading of the Holy Spirit. He knew that God would speak to the people about this situation and all it took was a combined effort of unity of the Saints to come together for the cause of truth.

The people prayed with earnest and great mourning for the revelation of the murderer of Sister Stray to be revealed. The Prayer Bands tied tightly around the waist of all the delegates present for the morning mass. Streams of

Yielding (2) Temptations

petitions began to flood the Mercy Seat of Christ, as the praise went up to the Holy Heavens like a sweet smelling savour. The hour of prayer was at its peak as the people strewn across the lawns of the Purley-Gate scenery opened their Bibles to reveal the new revelation of the scriptures. As Run-Tings gathered his spiritual pace on his leadership in interpreting the Gospel; he proclaimed victory in the name of Jesus to be the fundamental issue for opening up the mystery in the murder enquiry of Sister Stray. Although he found comfort in the Investigation Committee, he felt the only real solution could only come from the Throne of God. It was no simple task, no man doubted the ability of the unofficial Apostle; Run-Tings, as he spoke with the power and anointing emanating from God. He delivered a stern warning to all those who came for a show or just for speculation. He warned every individual of the danger to mock God in pretending and advised such a one to leave the camp before it was too late.

The Media crew took a careful note of the unofficial preachers words and began the process of publishing it in the Evening Standard due to be released in a couple of hours. <u>Headline News breaking on the front page.</u> **Unknown Preacher (Run-Tings) Predicts Murder Investigation To Be Unravelled By God's Intervention.** All the reporters and journalist laughed at the thought of God revealing the answers to a group of "Holier Than Thou" people, just worshipping on the grass in the middle of an insignificant town. But Run-Tings remembered Rev Tyson Junior 3rd's word, "Until the Proof is seen" then Run-Tings held his peace.

Sister "V" was tormented through the night, she thought of her emotional feelings towards Rev "T". She knew she was beginning to fall on an immoral

Yielding (2) Temptations

and slippery slope, and she knew that nothing could prevent this from escalating out of control; only prayer! She tried to focus on Heaven, but only returned back to Earth, she clutched her Bible with a vengeance, only to place it face down in ignorance. Then she remembered the Prophecy Run-Tings proclaimed to Rev "T", and pondered her next move. Outraged at being a feminine and emotional disposition of a woman, she wanted somebody to know about Pastors deceit and the deception fostered in his marriage and Pastoral duties in the church. She had to tread very carefully, not to arouse suspicion among the people. She felt bad knowing she'd been informed of Sister Fischer's husbands cruel act of adultery and with this information she would not be able to sleep well for the night to come. She had to do something, and she had to do it now!

Professor after his long and well earned rest; looked through the one-way safety glass and saw a sight he thought he would never see. Pastor Fischer now white as an Actors sheet; was foaming at the corner of his mouth and convulsing. The Professor pressed the Emergency Button for immediate medical assistance to the civilian. Professor Callme scratched his stubbled chin in dismay, thinking he was so sure he had him right where he wanted him. The probability that he over-stepped the mark in leaving the Pastor through the night with rodents led him to the conclusion that he had made a serious mistake.

Pastor Fischer was enjoying himself while convulsing with the morning phlegm. He began jerking, shaking himself as if he was pretending to be filled with the Holy Spirit, something that came easy with plenty of practice from his younger days. The uncontrollable Pastor Fischer exerted his best

Yielding (2) Temptations

performance yet. The Partial tape was removed, his hands were untied as he was hoisted and suspended in the air as they rushed to a more suitable room. The Pastor felt suddenly relieved that his plan was working to perfection. his eyes flickered open and shut like an automatic blind out of control gave him a clear view as to the direction of transportation. They led him to a room, 4 x 7, white padded walls embossed with white buttons, no bed, no linen, no music to soothe the day away; only a cushioned floor, warm and homely. Nurse Sergeant, (Male), with a Straight-Jacket, bombed into the room to apply the fasteners on his new restrictive apparatus. The phlegm ceased and the heart raced as Pastor Fischer realised he was setting himself up for an Asylum occupation.

The professor seeing the calamity unfolding before his eyes realised his star witness the informer could not be depended on for accurate information on current affairs. His aspiration and intended methods of interrogation could not be implemented, he had to put on the hat of an Investigator, and this was something he hadn't done for many years.

Rev Exodus rose up from his pre-paid, Charity hotel room with a headache. The morning was almost exhausted while completing his preparation for hygiene. He thought about his allied partner, Professor Callme, and decided to give him a call for an update. Viewing the business card that was exchanged the night before, Rev Exodus noticed the strings of letters after his name, and felt inferior in intelligence. A wave of sadness drifted over him as a moment of regret surpassed his thought for not furthering his education. A Doctorate in Theology would have been his ultimate achievement in life, if only they hadn't prevented him studying because of the lack of funds. He

Yielding (2) Temptations

lifted his head back to reality and dialled the number. The message rang out in his ears "the person you are calling is not avai...........!" Rev Exodus hung up the phone and decided to call later. Rev Exodus left his hotel room, too late for breakfast he headed towards the rendezvous point for the Executive Ministers briefing. He was hungry and irritated by the pounding headache; he was in no mood to stand for slackness in his Ministers behaviour.

There was an air of intrigue and suspicion in the conference room of the Evening News that morning when the news hit the headline press. The Editor in Chief demanded clarification on the story given about this person; "Run-Tings", otherwise his job and everyone associated with the story would be applying for the Dole increment for the foreseeable future. Witnesses were called and summoned with bribery to the National Press Officials. Minister, Judas King, would not have missed this opportunity for the world, so he craved and begged the National Bishop for a chance to take a break from his Ministerial Investigation of Evangelist Passover. Not giving full details of his participation with the National Press, he used his diplomatic tools to the max. Only suggesting his mere interest in seeing how the press got the information in the first instance he hooked Rev Exodus in believing he was still working under Spiritual cover. Rev Exodus gave him his eagerly awaited blessing, with this, Judas left in haste counting this familiar sin in pounds, shillings and pence. The News Editor was waiting patiently for Judas the National Executive Disciple of Christ, to point out "Run-Tings" in the crowd. The Editor, Harold Gainer wanted irrefutable proof in identification of the man. Judas King knew "Run-Tings" from his early days as a Minister and he thought it not wrong for him to approach him and shake his hands in respect for the hard work he was initiating with the crowd. Harold caught the drift and

Yielding (2) Temptations

examined the camera for available film, the batteries were low but it had just enough power for a couple of incriminating shots. The scene was set and Judas wanted desperately to get on with the charade in haste for the fortunes he was to behold. Thirty Thousand Pounds in real hard earned cash, he considered it a well-thought out, though demon driven intention, there was no time to lose.

Rev "T" locked the front and back doors of his luxurious apartment. With the telephones securely off the hook, he took a well-deserved rest from the calamity of the day. For once, peace and tranquillity flooded back into his life and brought back a long awaited order he so desired for his single occupation. No pressure, no demands, no surprises and no battering to be encountered by a brutal bloodsucking butchering lamb killer of a man. With the white and black check-duvet and matching pillows cases, he sunk into a world of unimaginable proportions. The mind instantly racing and inventing scenes so unbelievable it felt to good to be true. The twitching through the night left water-marks on the once white and black patterned check sheets that graced the Silent-Knight bed. His armed ached with a muscle contraction when hugging somebody too hard in his imaginary world. The pangs felt so deep and strong in his sleep still plagued him when he arose up in the morning. He could not quench the taste of "Love"! His sweat through the night overshadowed his ability to look cool in the early morning sunrise, he had to wash, and wash quickly before his jim-jams concealed stains of his emotional lust.

Judas King received the well-earned reward from the identification of "Run-Tings". "Thirty Pieces of Silver" in bundles of thousand-pound bills

Yielding (2) Temptations

were neatly wrapped within the bank seals, he was enlighten by the eyes of greed and fortune as a spirit of possession captivated the mind. He laughed to himself not knowing the implications on what was about to follow. The ground was beginning to open up, giving way to the precipice that would ensue, it was only a matter of time and his sand was running out within the hourglass.

At the National Evening News, the story was confirmed with a photo carrying the evidence of an association with a National Executive Minister, Judas king. The story passed the red-tape and cleared for mass printing. The new insertion done by the Editor in Chief brought a chilling and damaging twist on the entire story. Millions of copies collated for the international distribution to all national outlets, speedily making their way to the drop off zones. The thirty pieces of silver "Judas" was counting in private, the payment that was suddenly going to be his downfall. The exposure to the open world to his shame and the church's disgrace was about to consume the church into a new phase of mourning. It was a disgraceful act of deceit that was about to backfire. The hourglass was almost empty as the Evening Standard Newspapers were bought in haste by the news enthusiast.

Sister "V" spent the morning in fasting and prayer, asking God for a renewed cleansing. The emotional turmoil brought about through the night was far too much for her to bear. She had to take control of her life before the emotional immoral infection spread through her body like a plague of lust. Jumping hormones popping up on every occasion, seizing the little chance for a little demonstration. Her husband dressing for work walked through the passage-way whistling as he went by her door. He glanced in the spare-room

Yielding (2) Temptations

looking for pieces of evidence that would incriminate his wife for adultery and decided it was no use. "V" continued to pray with a lowered voice to her God, without giving away too much information for her husband to be suspicious. He decided he was going to work without having any breakfast; his intention was to check on his untrustworthy wife periodically.

Evangelist Passover was dumb struck when he realised he was missing vital pieces of purchase receipts that was so crucial for the tally. The miscalculation of his account balance sheet was overtly different to his bank statement totals. It tormented his mind for hours as he continued to rake the bedroom drawers in desperate attempts to find the answer. He prayed and asked God (while rummaging through the bedroom and living room sideboard) for mercy in his hour of greatest need. The heavenly angels looked on in disbelief while folding their heavenly hands across their chests. Evangelist Passover couldn't hear the heavenly music as they played the message to rely on God for his divine intervention.

Rev Exodus decided to take some decisive action. With Run-Tings firmly in the drivers-seat on the podium, Rev Exodus wanted to make his presence felt. Run-Tings spotted his National Leader approaching the stage and he announced to the crowd his National Bishop with a warm welcome that made Bishop Exodus feel, a little too good. The National Bishop without notes began to rehearse the scriptures with ease and simplicity. The focal point of his message was that we all should stand together in this greatest hour of need and God would answer all our prayers. (Even though he was not aware of the entire prayer request that went up to the Mercy Seat). He exclaimed that all his faithful Ministers from the National Executive office could be relied on for

Yielding (2) Temptations

the support necessary and to see this through to the end. Half the crowd began to jostle and shuffle pieces of papers that would bear some damaging news, as the other half praised God for the divine leadership on the Ministerial Leadership Party.

Sister "V" now in a spiritual mood wanted to join the all-night vigil for Sister Fischer. While waiting for the inner city bus that was due in 12 minutes, she glanced at the news-stands and read the new revelation that was about to hit the church and the investigating official like an atomic bomb.

Yielding (2) Temptations

Y (2) T

Scene 5

The rodents infested and overnight chill blades seemed like heaven to Pastor Fischer when compared with the asylum restraints of a straight jacket. There was no comfort, no place to reason or even to indulge in a simple conversation with mankind. He felt forgotten, thrashed out of society without any regards to his personal feelings and contributory ability. An outcast certified by medical engineers that could not tell the difference from a false prophet and a phantom pill. "Saving Grace" was now way beyond his limited comprehension. The feeling of failure and despondency crept in through his unconscious minds back door, without giving due warning to the rest of his unstable body, nor waiting for a response. Positive now turned to negative, with light turned back to darkness and love now vanished and hate crept into its place, the signs were now becoming familiar personality traits, and so Pastor Fischer was evidently labelled: a "Madman".

Pastor coiled himself into a foetus position, unrelaxed and pensive to every insect that crossed his path. He was becoming a nervous wreck. With no signs of improvement, it was downhill all the way for Pastor Fischer. The Professor visited a few times to check on the general progress of his once star witness,

Yielding (2) Temptations

now turned into a vegetable state, without a hope or a prayer. Pastor's now glowing red, bloodshot eyes penetrated the Professor with utter contempt. Anger and resentment filtered through his impregnable armour, as the eyes Pupil manifested its way to any suspecting individual. Every officer that worked in the Military Base was talking about the Nutty Pastor, who had caused the good name of the British Armed Forces to succumb to sorting out a church dispute. They were ashamed of him and every man who feed him bread and water protected himself with an outstretched truncheon at the ready.

An elderly man interrupted Rev Exodus while he was completing his masterful and spicy sermon. With grey streaked hair, and purley-white false teeth, six-foot and 4inches of pure bones that shone through his shirt collar where his Adams Apple plummeted to it's seasonal best, while holding the latest Headline Newspaper, roared with laughter at the National Bishop while pointing to his private parts. Rev Exodus spun around quickly to ensure no further embarrassment was centred on his zipper, but he didn't notice anything out of the ordinary. He slowly turned back around only to find dozens of Christian believers started shouting in full harmony. Judas, Judas, Judas, Judas.......

Judas King after he'd finished counting his thirty pieces of silver, viewed the uprising in the crowd from a distance. The Evening Standard newspapers were seen fluttering in the air as Rev Exodus searched for a sufficient answer for the believers. Rev Exodus then grasped the paper with both hands as one member of the crowd updated the National Minister of the headline. After reading the headlines, he began to scour the crowd for the unfaithful disciple, vowing to rend him into minute spiritual pieces for his deception. Judas

Yielding (2) Temptations

anticipating his next move ran to the nearest Newsagents to see the damming information for himself. The shopkeeper while presenting Judas with his purchase glanced back at the main photo clip on the front of the paper, and decided in his infinite wisdom to shout his offering of a damning curse directed at Judas the thirty pieces of Silver "King".

Evangelist Passover sat down to gather his thoughts. He had now swept every computer file and folder with a fine toothcomb and found nothing. Looking down at his hands stained in dust and grime, and picking the fragments of the cobwebs from in-between his fingers, he started to wonder to himself if it was all worth the hassle. The thought of a thriving business without a sound financial backing eluded any joy that would be generated in the coming weeks. For the second time this week (which was not unusual) he started again to pray.

Sister "V" paced herself on the walkway as she studied every word about the National Executive Minister Judas King. The name didn't mean much to Sister "V" at that point, but was rather curious to the level of his deception from an affiliating National Minister. The pennies finally dropped when she studied the evidence; and very slowly she then realised the implication it would have on every member of the Organisational Assembly. She sat and curled herself into a little foetus ball as she read the unfolding details. Her distrust in men in high standing, especially in the ministry was damaged yet again. Nothing that any man would say would convince her that they were genuine unless they were proved with infallible works and this included Rev Tyson Junior the 3[rd.]

Yielding (2) Temptations

Rev "T" still trying to relax and to forget about the world; was beginning to get quite comfortable. He dismissed his conscience that probed him to listen to the National News Bulletin, instead; he decided in his mind he was going to play a game of mind stirring chess, the box full of chess pieces lingered in the corner of his front room just waiting for attention. Rev "T" succumbed to temptation and darted to retrieve the box as he positioned them on the board with intense speed.

The news was breaking fast in the Passover restaurant of Judas King's betrayal. With the National Ministers whispering in the corner of the room to each other, it offered no clues to the onlookers of what was to become of Judas's faith. The crowd on the church ground started to disperse in great numbers in acknowledgement of Judas's downfall. Rev Exodus couldn't take the pressure any longer as he tirelessly collapsed on the hard benches at the front that supported the choir in peacetime. The National Ministers came running to the scene when they heard the thud that echoed through the grounds. An eager Christian; now well proficient in operating her mobile phone, called for an ambulance. A detailed account was recorded by the Emergency Services as they dispatched an ambulance that was soon on the scene. Elevated scenes of pandemonium swept through the church members as they surrounded the medical officers now involved in a desperate attempt to revive the life of the National Bishop. Tears of sorrow were evident on the believer's faces as they broke out in song. The Medical Officers crying out to the supporting Medical Teams for more supplies to hold together the hope of the National Ministers life. The look of helplessness on all Spiritual Leaders faces, as they turned their eyes to Heavens in an act of defeat, all because of

Yielding (2) Temptations

the absence of faith. A three-minute silence fell on the crowd as they took away the dead corpse of the National Minister to the Purley-Gate Mortuary.

the members of the local Purley-Gate church were Stunned into silence, they were called to an emergency meeting. The Host Pastor, Pastor Fischer was absent, now discredited by his position and involvement in current affairs and coupled with his sudden disappearance; The Church Council had now crowned Rev Tyson the 3rd to be the leader of the Purley Gate Assembly. The Pastors Council called sister "V" out of respect for her mature input in these trying times and decided that she would temporarily take the place as the Woman's President for Sister Fischer until she reached a full recovery.

Rev "T" looked at Sister "V" with terrified respect. (If only she knew what he was doing when Rev Exodus collapsed on the platform, she would not return a look with a favoured response.) She nodded with authoritative respect and sat down to listen to the agenda that was about to be chaired by the affiliating Church Officer, Deacon Gamble. The Deacon was swift and sharp. Not mincing his words, tearing to pieces any inkling of a chance for debate or democracy. He personally nominated Rev "T" to chair all future meetings for the foreseeable future announcing that if he Pastored well he would be guaranteed full Pastorialship of the Purley-Gate church. Rev "T" swallowed hard and couldn't contain himself with a sputter of excess saliva emanating from his mouth. It was clear the majority of delegates assembled had previously had a master plan without the knowledge of everyone concerned.

Rev "T" sunk into self emotional meditation and wondered why Sister "V" was there, was he chosen so quickly to bare the burdens of the people and to

Yielding (2) Temptations

take the blame? Was he announced leader of the Purley-Gate assembly because every-other member was too afraid to deal with the media? A likely thought, seeing nobody else volunteered to fly the flag of Spiritual freedom and Christian integrity. Rev "T" was the only man that was bright enough to tackle the problems that lay ahead. Deacon Gamble announced that they should all lay hands on the young Minister as he was ushered to stardom even in light of the crisis. Sister "V" was summoned to stand by his side and to hold hands as the Church Delegates prayed that these two young and mature individuals come together and work in God divine direction to steer the believers back to a spiritual place of prominence.

While the prayers was in a heated spiritual swing, Sister "V" looked at the side-view of her new leader and co-worker in Christ, she realised for the first time that she in fact had a serious problem. Holding his hands was the first real contact that was sustained for a long period of time. She knew in her mind that he was thinking about her; she knew in her heart that every twitch, every pulse that ran through his veins was connecting to her feelings for him. She couldn't let go of his hand, it would be too embarrassing, she kept the charade going for as long as possible but for Sister "V" it was becoming unbearable. Visions of her husband's yellow "Y" fronts pierced her mind and the drunk and disorderly behaviour played on her conscience as she summoned sanity to fall back into line. Rev "T" was more than a welcome break when she felt him squeeze her hand so tenderly, then sanity saluted to attention as Sister "V" returned to her sober mind.

Evangelist Passover scanned over the breaking news of the National Bishop premature death. Following every detail, he inspected the picture that

Yielding (2) Temptations

identified the individual concerned. He rummaged through the editors piece on the selling of the story of "Run-Tings", with Judas the "Iscariot" King incriminating the preacher in order to unravel the mystery on the former Prodigal Sister, mother of one "Stray". The Evangelist was intrigued with the spiritual matters that would bring about an unusual change in the ongoing investigation. Following the story with great interest, he wondered what kind of man would do this to the well known, and well-loved preacher Run-Tings in this way. His eyes were fixed on the piece that described the main culprit in the story. Judas King, the National Ministerial Executive that aided the National Leader who died in the wake of the deception. The Iscariot story in the Bible being fulfilled through real life's events, this manifestation through one of the National Ministers Disciples was a damning story. The implication and shock waves would reverberate through the assembly like a storm in a dry place. Judas King, how could he have done this to his own brother in Christ? How could he look anybody in the face again expecting genuine forgiveness for his actions? Evangelist Passover in his grieving for the National Leader began to summon up Love and Longsuffering for the guilty brother in Christ. He said to himself, we must learn to forgive, learn to forgive those who persecuted his own brother for his own namesake. He decided in his heart that he was going to be the one that would mortify his own self-feeling for the actions taken by the brother, and embrace him with a warm and heartfelt affection. He prayed in his heart for God to give him patience in all things and that he would show the congregation how to forgive and move on. He called Sister Chastity who was still in recess from the heavy duties performed in earlier event, but was willing to help the lost brother in need. The search was commenced by Evangelist Passover to find Judas and bring him before the Christian Jury for a spiritual trial.

Yielding (2) Temptations

Rev "T" felt good, consistently good. He could feel Sister "V" quivering in his hands and as he slowly anchored her hands in his firm clasp. He smiled outwardly as he felt her soft supple hands crumbled within his firm but loving hold. He slowly opened his eyes and caught her gazing into his sideburns, a look of acknowledgement greeting Rev "T" as he struggled to follow the prayers of the Leaders that placed the Church's faith in his ability to stay sober minded. Rev "T" was now in an emotional minefield. Littered with "Love-Bugs" all around his personality would most certainly cause undue stress on the Purley-Gate Saints. As if the people hadn't had enough problems, but the skies were the limit and he would have to learn to calm his sexual love pleasure, even if it was just for a season.

The prayer was finally over and the hands hastily separated. Sister "V" morally blushing and showing signs of immoral affection and were clearly evident in the eyes of Rev "T". Rev "T" was more composed, he had been through this before, concealing his feeling for another while performing important tasks for the public eye. Deacon Gamble shook Rev "T" hands with great ferocity and challenging him to act accordingly to his new unfound post. Eyes of desperation levied on the young preacher as the leaders were now expecting him to act. Rev "T" now positioned in a prominent status, wasted no time in dealing with certain subordinates. Starting with the untimely death of Sister Stray, he proposed, (then he re-adjusted his shoulders) and then ordered Deacon Gamble to search and find Pastor Fischer and report back to him immediately. Second; to locate the Professor Callme to the next meeting to sort out the confusion with the media. Three; for Sister "V" to work close beside him to look after Sister Fischer and to implement Secretarial duties

Yielding (2) Temptations

with immediate effect. Sister "V" nodded with a bemused agreement. The scene was set, Rev "T" was in full control and the woman he loves was by his side. He thought to himself, "how masterful and resourceful I was to choose such a wonderful secretary for my disposal", while Sister "V" decided in her mind she was not going to be an easy pushover for his manipulative control.

Rung-Tings was lost for words when the news of Rev Exodus finally reached him, while having lunch at the Passover restaurant. He wondered why everybody left in such a hurry when he was enjoying the starter, (Coconut Drops). That night, he called the newly appointed Purley-Gate Leader Pastor Tyson Junior the 3rd and offered his help and support in any matter he felt necessary. He offered a prayer to God while on the phone, asking God to distribute strength and wisdom in the days that are ahead. Pastor "T" reminded Run-Tings that the dream that he mentioned earlier should remain unspoken until proven. Run-Tings challenged the new leader with the wisdom that was being demonstrated. He was becoming rather concerned with the lack of spiritual guidance by the Holy Spirit due to the evidence not being manifested through the new leader decision in this matter. He realised he was fighting a losing battle, when Pastor "T" summoned silence, Run-Tings then held his peace.

Sister "V" visited the hospital in the early evening to check on the progress of Sister Fischer. The Doctors indicated to her and the immediate family that a slow progress would be expected. However, the Doctor offered no hope for a full recovery but was hopeful that all would go well. The Sister in law (Monica Fischer), started to weep when the doctor finished his explanation, although the information was hopeful and was not negative, Monica seemed

Yielding (2) Temptations

to gather negative vibes that stemmed from the inner weakness in male Practitioners ability in dealing with a woman's gynaecological problems.

In sitting down in the waiting area to interrogate Monica on her reasoning, Sister "V" used all of her diplomatic skills to manoeuvre through Monica's emotional minefield. Monica revealed to Sister "V", that Sister Fischer, (her younger sister) had cancer in the Womb some years ago, albeit she was crying out in pain for weeks, they gave no attention. Pastor Fischer begged the Gynaecologist to thoroughly examine his wife; otherwise he would be forced to make an official complaint. The Gynaecologist laughed at Pastor Fischer suggestions of any serious symptoms of Cancer but felt pressured to act in case he made an error on his judgement. The test returned a few weeks later (without giving treatment to her discomfort), and was proved positive for Cancer. A Cyst forming in the wall of the Uterus was later diagnosed as Cancer that required extensive surgery. Pastor Fischer filed his complaint to the Medical Tribunal and nothing was done to correct the wrong that was wrought on his wife.

The operation was to commence the following day and the church began to pray. Sister Fischer woke up the morning of the operation and felt excellent in her spirit. She told The Gynaecologist that she had not felt this good in weeks and that there was no pain for the first time. They still prepared her for the surgery only to find that when they opened her up, everything appeared to be normal without any abnormalities. Hence her confidence in Doctors deteriorated after that point. Sister "V" now understanding her misgiving in this situation assured her that her present condition was not and is not a pre-emptiveness of what's to come. Monica smiled with an un-assured

Yielding (2) Temptations

reaction but accepted her comments as genuine.

The vigil was dispersed from the main grounds of the church and was now centred in the Church hall with fewer believers. The main crowd went home after receiving the news of National Leader Rev Exodus death. It was an embarrassment, even the news broadcasters failed to cover the story they help to create. The media that initiated the damning story from the beginning said nothing. Judas was on the run and nobody could locate his whereabouts. But there were only a few places he could run to and Evangelist Passover was not going to let it rest until he was found.

Evangelist Passover prayed that evening, asking God to have mercy on Judas's soul. With a few Brothers encircling the Evangelist at the church, the Brothers were moved with compassion as they studied the genuine emotion the Evangelist had for Judas king's soul. The Evangelist prayed with a fervency never seen by him since he got saved and the Brothers caught on with the Spirit of Love and forgiveness as they huddled together in a time of spiritual intervention. Sister Chastity felt ashamed of herself for not acknowledging the signs of forgiveness, but when she saw the speed of Evangelist Passover, she had a renewed respect for the man of God. Sister Chastity called her prayer warriors to order, seeing the magnitude of the situation.

The Meeting commenced at twenty one hundred hours as the Prayer Ban team were all present and correct. There uniforms that were cleaned and unstained with excess moisture were quickly lubricated with oils that stretched the fabric beyond normal use. The aching muscles that rested from

Yielding (2) Temptations

the strains of the riot, quickly vanquished into infinity as the minutes translated into hours. Sister Chastity was a Leader and she would not allow Evangelist Passover to spearhead this campaign unless she was spiritually powerless to do so. Brother and Sisters in Christ trampled on Satan's Kingdom once again to find a solution to the whereabouts of the lost brother.

Two persons were on the run; one, for murdering of Sister Stray and the second, for selling the information to the media for thirty thousand pounds. Both had sinned and done demonic acts and yet the crimes would be punished differently according to state law if caught. However, the Christians had a dilemma, due to the nature of the crimes caused by the two individuals being very different; the sentences if not repented would be the same, Eternal Death. But the sentence Christians give in their hearts should only be Love. This was the problem that Evangelist Passover had to deal with when quizzed on his intention with the lost Brother. Evangelist Passover surmounted the task with wisdom the finesse. Controlling his temperament that was challenged only a few hours ago, he launched into the Bible with scriptures and facts about the abundance of love that should be present in every believer. He forgot about the running of the restaurant but he felt sure it was well looked after by his number one man, (Brother Spendeasy). Evangelist Passover never felt so spiritually uplifted for a very long time and he wanted to stay on this high podium forever, So much so he began to speak too much about his own personal involvement in forgiving others. Now he realised he had landed on dangerous soil, the scriptures dried up and he quickly climbed down from his high and mighty pride driven horse.

Judas, hiding in the cellar of the Purley-Gate church, felt safe and sure he

Yielding (2) Temptations

would not be found. Alter cushions and mouse droppings graced the floor as Judas made his makeshift bed for the night. The evening was cold and bitter with the winter chill spreading through the wooden floorboards. Judas knowing he had no covering, no coat to keep him warm through the night, cried with tears of despair on his face. The sombreness of his spirit numbed the pain from the cold as he drifted to sleep.

Rev "T" was striding with every breath. The visions of Sister "V" working closely with him warmed his spirit and desire. He thought about the authority he had and the perks of the job brought to his newly found post. He knew he would have made Pastor one day, after all it was why he studied for three years.

He remembered the words of his father when the image of Sister "V" was in view; "Tyson one day you will experience for yourself the pleasures of a woman, and it is nothing to be ashamed of". He definitely was not ashamed of how he felt about Sister "V", however, he had to keep it discrete in fear of the Pastors Council.

He wanted to meet Sister "V" and it had to be tonight. Tyson's inner man became enraged with unfulfilled passion that had to be quenched. Satisfying the lust coupled with power and authority carries a deadly sting to an unsuspecting young lady, but Sister "V" was at church praying for her sins and mourning for the death of the National Leader. Pastor "T" put on his official robe that enthroned his coat hanger for the momentous occasion. The day for Pastor "T's" crowning had arrived. Draped in black, white and blue, the Pastor curtsied in the mirror to check on the length of the robe. Perfect he

Yielding (2) Temptations

exclaimed to himself while clinching his Bible for an excuse to preach.

Pastor "T" left his home and whisked into the car without his garment touching the tarmac. He popped the keys into the required position and accelerated the right pedal to the ground. The engine roared with the 3.0 litre Toyota Supra driving machine. The wheels screeched so much it left a trail of smoke that covered the area the car was parked in, just a mist that faded into the night was the only trace left for the onlookers. Pastor "T" eyes focused and streaming with desire. He was on a high and he felt he could charm the panties off any woman, if he so desired. The red traffic light illuminated and he had to stop. The testosterone levels were peaking, all he wanted to do was to hold and kiss her like daddy had done so many years ago with the strange woman. He wanted to feel "V" in his arms, wanting his embrace. He couldn't wait any more, it had to happen tonight.

The church needed cleaning this night due to the brethren making complaints about the rubbish in the hallway. Sister "V" while praying saw Sister Alfonteen struggling with a load of cleaning materials from the side-room. Pastor "T" arrived at the church with an impressive stance, it shocked many believers but was welcomed by all, especially Sister "V". Sister "V" rushed over to her Pastor and gave him the thumbs up with her eyes. Pastor "T" motioned Sister "V" to a corner and whispered in her ear that he needed a dust cloth from the basement to clean some upholstery on the rostrum. Sister "V" nodded and moved in the direction of the basement.

Pastor "T" testosterone level was now measured by degrees as opposed to feelings. At a point of eruption he decided he should leave immediately to

Yielding (2) Temptations

engage Sister "V" in the basement for a moment's peace, but he had to shake a few hands from eager believers in the pew.

Sister Alfonteen was tired and Sister "V" wanted to do everything to help. She took the bucket filled with dirty water and detergents and told Sister Alfonteen to get the dust clothe from the basement. Sister Alfonteen made mention that the lights weren't working but she knew exactly were to look and Sister "V" then left her to empty the bucket in the kitchen.

Judas awakened   by the noise

Pastor "T" now craving for excitement lifted his garments and tiptoed down the stairs like he was thirsty for R-whites Lemonade. He could hear the footsteps in the basement as he heard Sister V(he thought) in the kitchen. Brilliant! All he could focus on now was the rules of engagement; a surprise attack to stun the willing victim was the best solution. Pastor "T" sprayed a breath freshener for extra confidence as he studied the outline of the "supposed Sister "V"", (Mother of Pearl). The animal instincts inside Pastor unleashed the inner emotions he had never felt before. His toes curled at the thought of wrapping his arms around this desirable woman. Supple and soft, each tender kiss fragmenting into a rose petal of desire. The cupid striking its bow in the wrong direction makes way for a great escape. The Jaguar Pastor "T" only inches away from Sister Alfonteen whispered in a deep manly tone "I was waiting for this moment for a very long time" as he embraced Sister Alfonteen with a "Hot Passionate Kiss".

Yielding (2) Temptations

Y (2) T

Scene 6

Professor Meseh Callme being inundated with the report from the Divisional Commander and the local Police Department found no time to interrogate the suspects for Sister Stray's killer. The Department of Defence seemed more interested in saving the image of the "Force" rather than dealing with a murder enquiry. This worried the Professor. Reading the news of Rev Exodus death shocked the Professor. He knew the fault was with the media and they would have to pay for the consequence of their actions. He had two bows he could use to strike the Department of Defence and he intended to use them to the maximum. The Professor called the church Secretary at 10 O-clock in the morning, but no reply.

A knock on his hotel door revealed a bunch of old men in worn out suits that smelt of mothballs. Deacon Gamble introduced himself and his faithful colleagues and the Professor ushered them into the room. Deacon Gamble rambled through pleasantries as though it served no purpose and began to instruct the eminent Professor to come to the emergency Councillors meeting scheduled tonight at 19 hundred hours. The Professor was intuitive to the request and he wanted to know the people who were in charge of the organisation in the absence of Pastor Fischer and the sudden death of Rev Exodus. So he accepted the invitation. Deacon Gamble stood up to leave with

Yielding (2) Temptations

the Cockroach deterrent odour and all the other delegates followed their leader to the door.

The Professor now cleansed from roach infestation open the window to bring a fresh perspective on the situation. He needed somebody good and reliable to work with him on the case. The complexities were growing by the hour and he needed professional help, but he was confused and had no answers. He placed aside all the reports and documentation that was related to the Government and decided he would mingle with the residents of the Purley-Gates to see what he could find out. He pulled the suitcase from the wardrobe to experiment with clothes so he could look casual. White T-shirt and khaki jeans and baseball caps were chosen as the tools for the job. The trainers and the greasy wave curls created by Dark and Lovely gave him the finishing touch. Cool!

The morning aroma of freshly cut green-grass, kindled the spirit of the naturist within the Professor. He loved the great outdoors. He once journeyed across the Argentinean border just to walk through the forest and mountain region of the Andes. There were no mountains in the Purley-Gate but the air was clean and pleasant with the natural movement of the birds gracing the skies. Peace and tranquillity he thought to himself momentarily had brought back precious memories once forgotten but now appreciated. He briskly paced the grounds, working out a strategy for his investigation. On remembering the meeting with the Late Rev Exodus, he had to see the Passover restaurant for himself. It couldn't have come at a better time seeing as he needed a good breakfast to quench his yearning for some home cooked soul food. And so he arrived at the place they called the Passover and stopped

Yielding (2) Temptations

just short of entering through the door just to look at the sign above the door for confirmation.

Nobody had ever cared about Spendeasy. He had always been an easy target; People used him, abused him, teased him and made fun of him. But for once in his life he found something he could do and do well. He could cook! People loved him for the technique he showed in his presentations at school. The pride he took in the preparation for Sunday dinner after church. He loved to see people eat. One of his great pleasures in life was to be a Chef and now he was working for the Passover, what a great opportunity to shine in the community and to be recognised by all his enemies that he was a man of honour. Another customer walked through the door as he raced to take the order from the strange but welcomed gentleman. The professor played it cool and acted trendy, like he wanted to blend in with great difficulty. Spendeasy could smell a rat from afar, seeing he was an expert in being bullied at school. He studied his accusers so much he anticipated when he was going to get the next beating, hence it gave him time to avoid any unpleasantness he might experience in the process. "Two eggs and Bacon, Sausage and chips please, immediately!" Spendeasy took one step back to have a good look at his pretender. In his mind he thought (who does he think he is?) demanding I make him "Two Eggs and Bacon, Sausage and chips" and on top of that, Immediately! The man is positively out of order and he needs to be disciplined. One thing Spendeasy learnt about getting revenge on people that upset him was to spike the food with something that is rather unsavoury. He replied and said certainly Sir, without a smile and walked away not bothering to ask if he wanted a drink.

Yielding (2) Temptations

The professor felt comfortable that he was making an impression with the lingo in the native tongue. He thought about the waiter not asking him if he wanted a drink, so he thumped the table with power and authority demanding service. Spendeasy returned, still not smiling but wiping his hands on the waist apron that looked immaculately clean. Spendeasy bowed in respect and asked what else can I do for you , Sir? The Professor shouted at Spendeasy that he wanted a drink and that he failed to ask him the first time. Spendeasy was deeply apologetic and clicked his fingers to usher another waitress nearby to bring a "Fresh" pot of tea. Ilda the agency waiter was very accommodating and returned with a fresh pot and the complementaries within minutes. The professor was satisfied as Spendeasy decided he was going to take personal charge with the preparation for the professor's breakfast.

Two Eggs! Spendeasy repeated to himself, as he wanted the pretender to have an exotic breakfast he will never forget. He cracked open the fridge door. It was huge, 6ft by 4ft wide and an attached freezer to match, reveal all the ingredients you could ever find in a restaurant. Spendeasy food oysters were at his blessed feet, Chicken, Oyster, Fish and Duck eggs that would make a difference to any exotic meal! On the side table in a soup dish were eggs that were not fresh, because they were out of date; 2 weeks out of date to be precise. Perfect Spendeasy thought. Sausages freshly made from the Cosha Shop around the corner came with a 3-day guarantee for freshness, no other choice. The bacon! well he thought he could spice it up just a little bit and the chips didn't need fresh oil.

This combination of the Spendeasy Special was ready to role. The Professor considered banging the table for attention but just as he was about to do so,

Yielding (2) Temptations

Spendeasy came out with a smile, showing his purley-white teeth for the first time. The professor was hungry now. My, my, the juices from the savoury flavour food touched his appetite and he was ready to eat whatever God put before him. Spendeasy placed a napkin on his knees like he was eating in some top West End restaurant but the Professor was grateful for the Que. The Professor wanted no prompting and he began to eat....mmm. Spendeasy thought; Yes! Eat man, eat...

Deacon Gamble being troubled to gather information on the whereabouts of Pastor Fischer resorted to questioning the Hospital Authorities to tell him of Pastor Fischer Exact location. The Chief Administrator located the document that was signed by the Military Personnel to admit him in care until recovery. He could offer no more assistance and no suggestions to overcome the problems of the lost patient. Deacon Gamble tried to place the blame on the hospital for negligence, but with this accusation the Administrator called for the Hospital security to remove him from the premises for behaving badly. Deacon Gamble tried to apologise, but they wouldn't have any of it and manhandled him by the scruff of his neck and elevated him through the A&E exit door. Deacon Gamble had failed yet again.

Pastor "T" was stunned and traumatised by the encounter of the night before, it had left scars that would mark him for the rest of his life. He felt helpless and motionless while he tried to sleep that night. He lay in his bed meditating on the encounter he had with a woman he believed to be Sister "V". The body with the curves on the woman surprised the Pastor beyond words. He couldn't speak; his tongue was fastens with the over eager passion of the woman in the basement. The woman seemed larger than life itself and he felt dumbfounded

Yielding (2) Temptations

that a size 14 woman could feel like a size 18-woman close up. He didn't question the physics; he had just enjoyed the moment, and a moment he will remember in history. He was turned on by the amount of moisture the woman in the basement had relinquished when touched by a man in the dark and this turned Pastor "T" on to do more secret rendezvous in the near future.

Sister "V" after getting a good night sleep, wondered why Sister Alfonteen had perked up with a noticeable vibrancy when she returned from the basement last night. She was singing and almost dancing like she had a new lease of life. Sister "V" asked her how she felt and she replied that she never felt better in many a year. Sister "V" thought to herself that if she knew she felt this good before she went to the basement, she would not have helped her with the heavy bucket full of dirty water, but decided to let it go. She was happy that she felt better within herself and she just put it down to the power of God reviving the body back to life.

Sister Alfonteen still on cloud 9 decided that on Sunday she was going to put on her best outfit for the new found lover in her life. She knew that Elder Standford (a Church Officer) had long since wanted to make a move on her, but she had waited for him to be masterful and take charge of the relationship. Only to find he was a pro-kisser that sent freshly minted kisses down her emotional spine. She was on fire and nothing in the world could ever persuade her that he didn't love her with a passion. She shopped that morning despite the mourning for the National Bishop and purchased a bright red lipstick and a matching broach to emphasise her mood. She wanted action with a vengeance and since Elder Standford had made the first move, she was ready to get into the rhythm of love.

Yielding (2) Temptations

The esteemed Professor left the restaurant after paying his bill a happy man. He did wonder why the waiter (Spendeasy), looked at him a little strange like he was expecting a tip. But keeping in the flow of the things he slapped the waiter and said, "food, cool maaan" and left the building. Satisfied and filled to the brim he wanted to have a rest and relax until the evening meeting.

The gathering was called to order by Pastor "T" now Chairman for the meeting. Sister "V" not on the same wavelength as Pastor "T" didn't read the signs of his approval for the way she was dressed. Sister "V" whipped out her notepad and pen to began writing the minutes for the nights session. Pastor "T" felt it appropriate for the eminent Professor Meseh Callme to make an introduction for his department of the MoD and any thoughts he felt relevant to the meeting.

The professor stood up. Fully dressed with the regular outfit his esteemed colleagues were very proud of, he demographically spoke with an eloquence that the Councillors felt uneasy with, because of their lack of understanding. Data was quoted to emphasis his facts and figures relating to the problems. The church councillors realised this was no ordinary man and each member nodded with approval, when asked if they can be relied on for their support.

Rev "T" followed the Professor with interest and excitement. For once he found a man he could relate to and he wanted to show the Professor that he was in the same league and class.

"We thank-you Professor for your valued contribution to the meeting and we

Yielding (2) Temptations

look forward to hearing your views on the matters that will soon be arising" the Agenda for the evening are as follows gentleman:

1. the Media intervention strategy
2. the church members conference
3. Pastor and Sister Fischer
4. Sister Strays killer
5. Rev Exodus death in relation to Judas King

Pastor "T" requested Deacon Gamble to pray asking God's leading on this part of the meeting and that every member would use wisdom and tactful diplomacy in this situation. The Professor opened one-eye out of respect for the intelligent way the Chairman was conducting the meeting.

Deacon Gamble prayed out loud without due care or correction to his words. Pastor "T" felt a little embarrassed that he had chosen such a man to ruin his image as a leader in the eyes of the Professor. But he remedied the situation as he carefully chose a scripture that would depict the moment of this critical situation to the letter. The professor followed the comments made by Pastor "T" with great interest as Pastor "T" placed emphasis on his words to give extra clarity to his audience. Five minutes passed by when Pastor "T" felt justified he had covered the translation of Biblical scriptures into today's reality.

The past meeting minutes was read by Sister "V" as every eye was on the young and beautiful feminine specimen. Her words echoed through the room like essence in a seasoned kitchen. All noses and lips in unison were raised in

Yielding (2) Temptations

a perpendicular fashion to incite agreement. Pastor "T" asked if the minutes could be accepted and hence the need to motion for total agreement by two members of the board. Elder Standford first moved for the minutes to be accepted and then seconded by Deacon Gamble.

The first item on the agenda was the Media Intervention.

Elder Standford jumped to his feet as if he eagerly wanted to say something. Rev "T" cooled his heels as he felt it necessary to give a brief synopsis to the current situation.

"A few days ago this was a quiet and beloved town and people got along just fine (he suddenly realised he needed to use language that would compliment his level of intelligence in the presence of the esteemed Professor). The Media forced the issue of our Pastor Fischer's moment of indiscretion into degrading proportions. They highlighted the position with the Military with great accuracy and formed an alliance with the Department of Defence and most of all placed the whole Church Administration into disrepute. This cannot be allowed to continue. We have to be seen with evidence to be taking charge of the situation without this Media control". All Member heads hummed with total agreement, Sister "V" looked up and smiled while completing his last masterful sentence. Pastor "T" felt he had the bull by the horns and he was ready to rock and roll. Elder Standford still heated in his seat to say something was now allowed to stand and deliver his thoughts on the subject. All eyes glanced on the Elder as he captured the attention with his all white hair and sideburns to match, the suit immaculately tailored to his personal style and pose and ready to issue his well thought out presentation.

Yielding (2) Temptations

"Even though we may feel the Media is to blame for the outrageous way they proclaimed or printed the story, it was factual and no fabrication to any information was evident. We cannot blame a system for accountability; however, we can remedy how we behave. I feel there is an undercurrent in all of this, something sinister and unpleasant was or is happening to our leaders that would have caused these strings of catastrophes to happen in the first place.... Pastor "T" stood to protest but was told to sit down by the Elder in respect for not finishing his statement. Pastor "T" felt small and saw the need to exercise his authority again. He had never been challenged before and Elder Standford was a force to be reckoned with. Sister "V" glanced at him while capturing all the evidence of this humiliation on paper. He casually glanced over her shoulder to see what she had written of the incident. He began to read and noticed that she was very accurate in the minutes. Ever word and phrase was noted like a script in a church play. She looked at him in bewilderment and he took it badly. Pastor "T" felt hot under the collar. War with saints in an important meeting with dignitaries present daunted him. Elder Standford rubbed the salt in the wound as he commented that church today with young people having lost respect for the "Elders in the faith. A new structure of order and respect should be implemented with immediate effect before the church comes down to nothing. All the elderly members, which were the majority barring 4 shouted "yes I agree" There was no need to vote democratically, the shouts were enough. Pastor "T" thought that Elder Standford had finished, not realising he was just getting started. Elder Standford ruffled his tailored suit as he began to mastermind his stamp of authority in the meeting. The older members were in a state that was almost euphoric. Jackets backed off and sleeves rolled up like they were expecting a

Yielding (2) Temptations

fistfight. Pastor "T" had to act, and he had to do it right now.

A cry of overwhelming pain swept the room as the Professor crashed to the floor clutching his stomach in agony, and unceremoniously releasing his poisoned bowels in a watery flood. His cheeks went an agonising red with bulbous eyes to match. The squeals and whaling of pain reached all the individuals that were pursed ready for a heated debate that would have lasted through the night.

Pastor "T" moved into First-Aid action. Councillor's stood idly-by watching every action the young leader administered in the meeting room. Possessed with a nurse-like demon he staggered to the nearest phone only to find it was a payphone, even for emergencies. He was confused with their reasoning but he was on a mission that he could not afford to fail. His triumph over this to save the Professors life would obviously put him in good stead for partnership. The ambulance was scrambled to the scene when a detailed account was given to the medical team on the emergency line. The Paramedic commended him for his accuracy as they pump his stomach for the enduring acid and food poisons that was causing so much pain. The unpleasantness in the room was evident by the Elders holding their noses, and the uncleanness of the air as the gasses circulated into the atmosphere with a vengeance; causing many to leave the stenching room. The emergency team junior administered an Enema to an already vibrating organ which was obviously active in the presence of everyone left in the almost vacated room. Handkerchiefs were passed around the neighbouring room when the foul and lingering unpleasantness magnified itself into an unbearable stench. The mothball odour that dominated the room before had vanished; probably gone

Yielding (2) Temptations

back to the cupboard praying for the spring to come. The pain was easing and so was his organ. Every wind that passed through brought a greater sense of relief for the carrier but brought a greater presence of foul play for the receiver.

Pastor Fischer was not allowed to stand in his confined military cell. He stayed In a crouched position for most of the night without supervision. Still strapped into his straight jacket that gave no allowance for upper muscular movement, he kicked frantically like a footballer who has lost the plot. The food was served without a knife and customary fork. He had to use his head like a dog, twisting and turning to angle the supposed meat of unknown species into his mouth gave Pastor Fischer no easy task to survive this living hell. But he was determined to right the wrong he had done, but he struggled to find a moment to execute his intentions. While fumbling with the tough meat handed to him on a platter, he heard laughing that disturbed his already warped drugged mind. He wasn't thinking straight. He could not tell the difference from reality to fiction, however hard he tried to focus. He heard men banging tables in rages of laughter, although he could not prove this was actually happening, it made him growl all the more for the soldiers secret viewing entertainment. Pastor Fischer was being made a private spectacle and the soldiers loved every minute of it.

The soldiers loving every minute and being unsupervised for a long period of time took advantage of the situation. They teased Pastor Fischer with food on a string, tough meat that could not be chewed and vegetables that hadn't been cooked sufficiently by a Military Chef. They all wanted a piece of revenge and desired to teach the so-called loving brother in the Lord a good time. One

Yielding (2) Temptations

said he was like Jesus without the power but another one objected because he was an Atheist and didn't believe in him. A scuffle broke out among the soldiers about the principle of Military behaviour, whilst others left the room in disagreement. A division in common standards was evident in the ranks, however feeling for the common Christians were in general quite agreeable in the majority. But Pastor Fischer was an exception to the rule; he could not be trusted to lead an innocent flock to the altar to pray for their sins when it was so evident he had many things to repent of himself. A long cold winter night loomed over the horizon once again as the soldiers clambered back to their respective barracks. Pastor Fischer was to be left alone for another lonely night without torment and edible food.

Sister Chastity praying consistently knew that Pastor Fischer was in trouble. Calling her trusted Prayer Ban group, she wasted no time in spiritually investigating the sudden disappearance of their once infallible leader. Talking to Run-Tings she gathered that something was a-foot and was suddenly determined to get to the bottom of it. The night grew dark and mysterious, every hour in prayer brought forth new ideas and theories into the minds of the prayer warriors. Sister Chastity leading with the power of the Holy Spirit rejected all the thoughts that were not confirmed by Gods approval. Thus hence, it was now confirmed before the morning light, that Pastor life was containing a mystery that needed to be unravelled and dealt with before the church, before things would improve in the Purley-Gate church. Sister chastity was not a fool. She called Elder Standford on his phone and realised that he was unhappy for not finishing his masterpiece in the meeting. She told Elder Standford her new findings. Elder Standford was delighted in his heart, he knew this must of been the move of God. Sister Chastity made certain

Yielding (2) Temptations

recommendations. Elder Standford listened intently as Sister Chastity Like the novel "Murder She Wrote" unveiled her master plan. Elder Standford clapped his hands in muffled glee knowing he could now prove Pastor Fischer was involved in something sinister and ungodly. He replaced the handset down into position as he thought about the execution of sister Chastity's Godly plan.

The Professor woke up the next morning with a pain in the rear. He felt a surge of the urinal adrenaline that caused him to rush to the nearest public or private convenience. His gown was stained with yellow fever "he justified the yellow fever because he was so hot under the collar with bowel pressure". He pushed Nurses aside with one hand while holding his private bursting parts with another. A Ward Sister was going to hand the Eminent Professor a specimen bottle and changed her mind when she saw the leakage already evident on his apparel. She decided to take on his pace to lead him to the nearest toilet, cursing the cleaner along the way for not being efficient in cleaning the mess created by the previous Patient. The Professor reached his destination and collapsed on the seat while observing the urinal trail, like gun-powder fused to explode at the toilet door. Then the Professors Bomb was delivered with Precision and Ease as the Nurse vacated the area now contaminated with methane gas. The cocktail created by Spendeasy was so abdominally dangerous that it made the Professor exhausted just by the thought of going to the toilet alone. The Nurse who were paid by the National Health Service, thus paid for by the tax payer, giggled at the thought of the Professor breaking uncontrollable "wind". But the Ward Sister was having none of it and screamed at the Orderlies to get on with their jobs and clean up the mess immediately as she wiped her shoes from the urinal trail.

Yielding (2) Temptations

The Professor still passing frequent bowel waters visited the men's room every hour. He noticed on the notice board Mr Fischer name that that was still etched on the board with rubbings out around it. A strange looking woman was interested in Pastor Fischer inscription. He hobbled closer to glance at her immaculate figure. Five foot and three inches of woman, dressed in a knee length pastel coloured skirt and a matching waistcoat, catwalked through to the reception desk. The professor was taking mental notes. Shoulder length hair slightly curled at the bottom and a single dimple on one cheek gave rise to a pleasant rose- petal smile. The Professor bending on breaking wind, positioned discretely on the corner was within earshot to hear what was being said; But the Professor was on an instinctive intuitive mission. Not only were her looks physically attractive but her motive for being there aroused his senses of suspicion to something new.

The mystery woman quizzed the receptionist about the missing Pastor Fischer but was told she could not divulge such information only to a family member. The Mystery woman remained cool but felt provoked. Looking either side of the room for clues gave her no comfort so she left without saying, goodbye. The receptionist glanced at the winded professor and had a curtailed smile on her face.

Pastor Fischer was still hungry and desired some Earl-Grey tea to break the hardness created by his lower abdomen. Pain in his lower regions was experienced when he tried to release himself without the use of hands to caress the congested area. He had to do something otherwise he would be forced to blow, and no matter what gases contaminated the confined area, he

Yielding (2) Temptations

hoped he would live to breath fresh air in the long and not to-distant future.

The mystery murderer wanted information on the whereabouts of her lover. She feared something rather underhanded was being presented before her, so she cleverly thought out a reason for his sudden disappearance. Maybe this was done to flush out any other suspecting accomplices to the murder of the late Prodigal Sister Stray, or to break the Pastor's resistance in presenting the reason for his sermon that Christmas morning. The murderer was going to play it cool and not expose her cards on the table for all to see. She knew within herself that Pastor Fischer wouldn't expose her to the world unless his life was threatened beyond endurable pain and she was sure he was not going to be tortured for something they could never prove.

The soldiers were not happy. Smothered with white filtered tissue and a nose mask working in tandem, presented an enormous task for the brave souls that had to do the cleaning up. The buttons that once graced the padded room with sophistication and style was now embossed with gravy browning coloured streaks that had not lived up to the after taste. Surges of rear-raw-power filtered through the tightened straight jacket with ease and devastation, the likes never seen before by the military force. Pastor Fischer as far as the soldiers were concerned was striking back with a deadly force that would stain every soldier's moral for a very long time.

Yielding (2) Temptations

Y (2) T

Scene 7

Sister Alfonteen circuited the fashion stores with enthusiasm and relentless energy. She tried on many outfits that would catch the eyes of her new-minted pro-kissing lover. Every time she looked at herself in the mirror with her new designer outfit, she remembered the feeling of love and affection that surpassed all of her past feeling of other experiences. She truly adored his masterful character and vowed to release more passion juices in the next private encounter. A carnal demon was getting the better of her without her detection. She had given into carnal pleasure and self-satisfaction without due care and control. Parading all the clothes purchased that morning on the bed made her almost ready to approach any emotional situation. She glanced again at the mirror and saw newly recognised flaws in her makeup that needed immediate attention. Frantically pursing through her diary she found the number for the most expensive makeover artist in town. "J B, (Mr\Miss Junior Brown)". Sister Alfonteen made the appointment for that afternoon.

On arriving at the private residence of "JB", Sister Alfonteen needed help in translating some of the strange artefacts on display before her in the room. A picture of a beautiful woman, but certain parts was clearly evident as a man, a classic figurine of a black Ibonian woman embracing reality with another woman dancing in tandem. The music transcribed and aired by some unknown author filled the room with confusions and many unanswered questions of originality. Sister Alfonteens mind was certainly wondering, so

Yielding (2) Temptations

she began to refocus on the reason for being there; Elder Standford, and with this thought everything that was unanswered seemed to fall back in its rightful place.

Elder Standford was elated in his heart with the up-to-date news Sister Chastity provided. He knew secretly that something was happening to Pastor Fischer and the leadership Council, excluding himself of course. The Elder prayed that same night with passion, asking God for guidance to unleash this deadly information missile about Pastor Fischers ungodly behaviour while in office. Elder Standford saw his chance to lay the groundwork for his "planned" appointed position of Chairman of the Councillors Board, of course he would begin to execute his intention to discredit Pastor "Ts" authoritative position as leader of the Purley-Gate Assembly with immediate effect. Elder Standford needed a new suit, a suit that would catch the eyes of every believer to indicate that he was certainly whiter than white. And what would be more appropriate than a white suit with a Purley-White shirt and a white Tie to match. Perfect he thought! He rummaged through his tie-rack to find a tie that would meet up to the specification, and failed.

Elder Standford insisted with a storekeeper to furnish him with the most elegant and dashing white suite in the store to match. The Managing Director pensively listening to all the customers who came through the doors had now found his prized target. He instantly brushed the desperate assistant aside; with the Assistant feeling distraught that he lost out on commission his boss was so reluctant to giveaway. The nametag on the Managing Directors breast flashed with the illuminating fonts, "Dr Preddy".

Yielding (2) Temptations

Elder Standford felt at ease with his new Fashion Consultant. A sense of pride filled his ever-increasing ego when he saw the logo of distinction; it brought about a light step in his shoes as he was ushered to the elite suits section. The distressed assistants new customer needed a pair of socks in a certain colour, his job was on the line if he failed to suppress the rage, so he humbly obeyed with gritted teeth, the customer's request for service without giving a smile.

Elder Standford now on cloud nine with his esteemed humble servant; surveyed the array of fascinating clothing that graced his eyes in wonder and amazement. His heart felt elated that he can now achieve his ultimate challenge for supremacy in the Officers Board. He posed to himself in the mirror as the white suite draped his masculine slim but tall frame with an untarnished flaw. Satisfied that he found his complete outfit he strutted in front of the enlarged door mirror with the shirt and an amazing red ignitioned tie for subtlety. His forever-Flexible friend took care of the damaged without even recognising the damage it inflicted on itself. Elder Standford was a shrewd and wise man financially, but on this occasion he was going to release his purse strings whatever damage it caused on his credit status, this was to the Directors delight and joy.

Pastor "T" was completely in control of the situation as he eased into his car with a confident step. Still feeling the moisture of Sister "V" lips; which was implanted so firmly in his mind, he couldn't wait for the next encounter. Relishing the moment for a closer intertwining of the heart he stopped at the Off License to give his tongue a minted flavoured texture. As he soothed his tongue in caressed appeal and approval, he replayed the moment of sheer passion excreted some days earlier.

Yielding (2) Temptations

Pastor "T" followed the news-broadcast with difficulty given by an Anchorwoman that was ill-prepared to deliver a message to the nation. She fumbled through her notes on the radio with such unprofessionalism, Pastor "T" turned it off. His mind was made up. He had to see Sister "V" before the Sunday Gospel service. The Councillors Board had decided it was time for Rev "T" the 3rd to stamp his authority in the new position as Acting Pastor. But Deacon Gamble failed to notify the said minister in advance.

Pastor "T" was relentless in trying to find ways in capturing Sister "V" once again for a moisturising exhibition. He tried to phone her home, but was unsuccessful. He drove around her home and stopping short of the street she lived on, so not to be recognised by a straying member of the church. With a carefully prepared note that indicated an urgent Officers Meeting starting at 2100 hrs, and not to forget to bring the minutes taken from the last Councillors Board. It was delivered with speed and agility the Royal Mail organisation would have been exceptionally proud. The "Rev" skilfully retraced his steps back to his vehicle and vacated the neighbourhood travelling just within the city speed limit.

Being a prepared man that he was, he started working on his sermon for the Sunday morning service. Many thoughts crossed his mind as he prayed asking God for a divine message to inspire the people and the inquisitive audience. It was a challenge that Rev "T" wanted to aspire too. People believed in him and he needed to show the world who was the new boss in this church, a stirring message that would touched the hearts of every believer, even the unsaved.

Yielding (2) Temptations

Sister "V" capturing the little sun that was left in the day dedicated herself in meditation on all the recent events that had taken place in the last week. She volunteered to look after the official church documents until a new permanent National Bishop was appointed. Tremendous pressure was on her young shoulders in the coming weeks that lay ahead. She decided to seize whatever moments she had to relax, knowing that it would be short lived. A postman working late in the afternoon dropping mail through her door interrupted the stillness of the room briefly, but she paid no attention to the intrusion. The phones were plugged out of its socket in fear of other reprisals like the late prodigal Stray and undisciplined brethren. "V" gathered her senses and was feeling herself once more. Savouring every minute of silence and tranquillity, she read her Bible with renewed confidence. The revealer of truth inspired her mind as the time went by without a care in the world.

Pastor "T" the 3rd was pacing up and down his office with impatience for the desired Word for the Sunday Morning Service. He placed the Bible on his chest as he lay on the floor and reminisced on his soul-tie Sister Voluptuous "V". The moment the inner thigh caught his attention, the image grew larger in greater detail on inspection from memory. The delight and enticement of intertwining his powerful manly desires brought a heat-wave of emotion that resembled an ungodly carnal Tsunami. The epicentre of the emotional quake happened hours ago, now the waves of the past recollections were flooding his soul with ferocity and spiritual destruction. No resistance, No barriers of prevention entered the mind of the young captive Reverend. It was at this point the Rev "T" the 3rd had submitted to the cross and had laid all his concerns on the Mercy seat of Christ. The Reverend rose from his knees with his eyes firmly fixed to heavens and outstretched arms……

Yielding (2) Temptations

The birds sang with melody and purpose this Sunday morning. The hustle and bustle of the street life generated a warmth of friendship among dog-handlers as they released their four legged friends out into the open wild. A little poodle was seen wearing a technicolored coat, poor thing, he was preparing for a grand theatre performance. The Poodle was shivering by the wayside as the owner had seen fit to light-up a cigarette to relieve a precious moment. The Poodle was not impressed, occasionally glancing up sideways nonchalantly and demanded attention to release him from his suffering of inappropriateness.

Pastor Fischer's classic demonstration of his acting ability was creating a whole new depth of troubles he would find extremely difficult to overcome. The white press studded buttons and cushioned surrounding couldn't comfort his aching soul. Memories from the Memoirs of his past mistakes flooded his mind as he squeezed his shoulders furiously to loosen the grips of the straight jacket.

He couldn't understand why Sister Fischer had neglected to attend to his manly needs. Potently Primed and ready for action, he had had many moments of dissatisfaction; all this frustrated the Local Bishop to a point of anti-climax. The midnight silent-ness of in-activity in the bedroom created a vacuum of emptiness Pastor Fischer found unbearable. He probed the open market field of sin for some solace and physical fulfilment: It was at this point he became a marauder of the female species in the Carnal Kingdom.

He found a woman, a woman that pleased and always ready to respond with a

Yielding (2) Temptations

tease, she found and explored his inner adolescent manly-hood with rampant and un-repentant enthusiasm. This excited the frustrated Pastor Fischer to a point that he became reckless in his private endeavours when his rendezvous was executed behind is wife's back. To the Pastor's delight and joy he enjoyed the warmth of a full bodied reciprocating woman. She seemed to demand stamina and patience in every department of their interactive activities. The fun he experienced was endless and the encouragement she awarded to him, he regarded as "Priceless".

Pastor Fischer felt alive when in her presence, which exuded the dominant beast he never knew he had within. predator instincts rose up in him early in the morning to devour the victim's pure undiluted carnal flesh; it fused his appetite for more love and unconditional devotion.

While focusing on her slender Ebonian features he curled in a breached birth position on the cushioned white floor and cried. His energy waned in the pangs of helplessness as the guardian watched on with inquisitiveness. The wardens who patrolled the ward at night listened carefully to the sounds of woe that emanated from the restricted room. On this night one of them stopped and heard the whispers of a dialogue coming from the single-tongue. He shook his head from side to side while clicking both fingers in unison, saying "God Forbid!!"

Pastor Fischer had to speak, but he thought he was talking within himself. This loss of control and self discipline was becoming more frequent throughout the day. He thought about his one-love, and then he bellowed out the condemnation and accompanying complementary scripture to back it up.

Yielding (2) Temptations

The One-Time Minister started to believe he was in the right place for his uncontrollable condition and losing his sanity may have been a far-gone conclusion.

Sister Alfonteen now primed to touch the heart of the unsuspecting soul of Elder Standford, adorned herself in a beautiful black and red exquisite negligee, complimented with the black fishnet stockings that accentuated the calves of a mature woman. She twisted her hips slightly to reveal the posture of the stocking line, she was satisfied it demonstrated the right message for the desired on-looker. The dress welcomed Sister Alfonteen on the mannequin while displaying the mother of pearl necklace. She smiled satisfyingly as she lifted the mother-of pearls and tested the compatibility with the negligee. She momentarily thought about wearing a cross, but changed her mind in conclusion it would send out the wrong message to the right person.

The dress was a crimson red with a plunging noticeable neckline. Its design was to embody a woman with assets that needed to be displayed for a purpose of magnetism. Sister Alfonteen loved this dress, she felt young and vibrant; just picturing herself strutting down the isle with her imaginary man by her side gave her the goose bumps. The hours was being counting for the impending and inevitable encounter. Her heart was beating erratically in moments of reflection of her last surprised minted session. She was poised and ready to demonstrate to her lover, that the next level had already been breached, this incumbent boat of emotion was about to flow into the ocean without a paddle…

Meanwhile, Elder Stanford had unfinished business with the Councillors

Yielding (2) Temptations

Board. Early Sunday morning he felt the need for clarity and emphasis in his mannerism and dress-code. The uncompleted performance while on a high in the meeting needed to be finished. A statement was essential if he was to carry out his plans. He pondered on the appropriate fashion message needed to convey the point to his fellow compatriots.

After much mental thought he had chosen black, complimented with the red-flamed ignitioned tie, he felt comfortable to deliver a message of importance. With his polished black shoes and serrated red designed breast kerchief Stanford believed he was ready to go into conflict with any opposing officer.

Elder Standford was too proud to be attached to any woman. Too many emotional attachments would limit his ability to fulfil his dreams. He wanted "Power", power that could propel him into the high realm of Christian stardom. The only paradigm that could persuade the Elder to take on the insurmountable challenge of engagement of the opposite species; if the qualified woman of distinction carried the name "Olive" promising submission, humility and a promise to obey the Head of the House, in all things. There was no room for negotiations with Elder Standford; this was his "LAW".

A woman called Sister Alfonteen seemed to be keen on him, the shifting of the eyes and occasional un-necessary brushes with the hand while greeting, gave away any secret emotional feelings of desired future attachment. Standford kept his distance with such women; he had seen too-many Preachers and inspirational leaders fall into the wrong hands and been excommunicated, just

Yielding (2) Temptations

for showing an interest. He wanted to keep his character portrayed as Whiter than White and he intended to dry clean his Purley White suit just to emphasize this very point.

Sister Alfonteen in crimson red strutted to the Purley-Gates with excitement and intrigue. She could feel the Passionate Juices of Elder Standfords minted kisses discharging into her welcome cocktailed soul mixed with a hint of lemon and ice. She felt hot and the ice was melting fast, if the juice wasn't flowing soon, the ice would dissolve and all they'll be left would be the bitter lemon-aftertaste of failure. She lifted her head high and clicked her heels in a frenzied anticipation to go that extra mile to reach her ocean.

The Secret lover of Pastor Fischer was pensively waiting for the update from her underground source. Jango eventually arrived back in her singles apartment after 10am with a note. It read! "Target (X) surrounded in a classified military base, No informants available to provide rescue operation-due to lack of general intelligence". Jango was ordered by the Lover to leave and return to his homeless bunker. The Lover reacted sharply to the cul-de-sac dead leads by throwing her half finished wine glass through the patio opening, the glass shattering into pieces with fragments falling from the storied building into the greenery below.

The lover couldn't stand this feeling of inadequacy, knowing her one-love was somewhere, defenceless and without her shield to depend on. Twisting on her king-size bed with uncertainty, she launched and grabbed her laptop to view the latest local news.

Yielding (2) Temptations

Browsing concertedly for ideas and clues of her missing Lover, she found a lead. The Passover Restaurant featured quite a few times in the Old News Section on the Webb. She remembered clearly Pastor Fischer talking about a young bright boy called "hmmmm-Spend-Spend-Spend, Spendeasy! That's it "Spendeasy".

The moment of his appearing at the Purley-Gate, would come like thunder and true revelation from heaven. Pastor "T" the 3rd rose out of his bed in a sweat. His nights experience was taking it toll with a vengeance from the excess moisture displayed on the sheets. He propped himself up, turning his head 180 degrees from side to side while focusing on his pillow, the night was evidently hot and upsetting. He closed his eyes…

The sultry heat of the beach inflamed the passion felt between The Rev and Sister "V". Stimulated by aspirations and affections, they embraced. The heated connections travelling through their veins with desire and passion. "T" junctioned when the Priority had to be changed for "V"'s right-of-way. The passage was cleared from all other unnecessary obstacles. The Rev engaged his gears of motion when he saw the anxiously awaited green-light. He pinned his accelerator to the floor for maximum thrust and power. Sister "V" saw the beast of Reverends gear change. Moving swiftly into second gear, she turned on the air conditioning by cooling his body with a tender kiss to the ear. At this point The Rev was manoeuvring in his 3rd gear, when…….He opened his eyes.

The feline stalked the hairy creature tucked closely behind the pew. Feasting

Yielding (2) Temptations

on the crumbs of biscuits left over from the Lord Supper weeks earlier, the four legged creature decided to run across the pulpit floor, warily avoiding possible danger. The Master Stalker crouched between the seating areas of the pew avoiding eye contact with the desired luncheon meat. Dripping with a ravenous appetite, it lunged forward with its paws fully outstretched for capture. The vermin's sixth active sense steered left instinctively to miss the cat's claws of death. The rat increased speed on the curve put distance between the killer and the option of continued life. The felines dogged attempt to capture this specifically aggravating rat aroused the determination to continue the hunt another day.

The Rev was in a periodical emotional spin. Forgiveness then sanctification and anointing were needed in order to dispel the sins of the night. After the three processes were complete, the carefully arranged robe of authority and prestige was awaiting the new leader. He thought about this long awaited moment and smiled. The message was ready and he was now ready for the mantel of leadership to take active effect with the church's backing. It was a pivotal moment in his life that he would treasure and never forget. He recited the 23rd psalm to himself, "forgetting all the things left behind (except Sister "V") and pressing forward to the mark of the higher calling".

Spendeasy was a valued Usher for the Purley-Gate Church; he was required to arrive at church early every Sunday morning for the preparation for the service with Evangelist Pass-Over. The cross-bodied banner and name-tag clearly identified his ranking and position in the Ushering department. Evangelist spotted this young man a few years ago. With a low self esteem and confidence he decided to give the boy a chance to develop his skills. To

Yielding (2) Temptations

the Evangelist delight and joy he could cook and cook well; a true asset to the Pass-Over Restaurant.

Spendeasy on inspection of the church pulpit found crumbs of biscuits with evidential paw marks on the parquet floor. Aunt May the cleaner was arriving a little later than usual and was hanging her coat in the Janitors quarters. He motioned her assistance pointing out the need for the extra buffing on the concerned area. Spendeasy knew the crumbs on the floor must have been there due to a mouse or God Forbid a Rat. Stretching across Aunt May's shoulder he grabbed the rat poison and sprinkled it around strategic corners and crevices of the pulpit and church entrance corner. For an extra deterrent, a mouse trap was laid inside the pulpit base with a few crumbs on top for entrapment.

Evangelist Pass-Over arrived some minutes later. He brushed his hands along every edge and table-top for dust particles and found no discrepancies. Giving a well earned thumbs up for Spendeasy's effort; he proceeded to the rostrum for the choirs chair positioning and musical electrical inspection. He glanced to his left and spotted a black fierce looking cat, arched and ready to scratch; the Evangelist cornered the beast with an enlarged print Bible used for major sermonettes in the Ladies Ministry. Tucking down to a Sumo position and the Bible stretched out, he grabbed the upper collar of the black cat and hastily dropped the Bible to open the base church window to release the unwanted intruder. Satisfied he'd done an excellent extraction, the Evangelist went to the Pastor's changing room to remove the cat hairs attached to his trouser and shirt sleeve.

Yielding (2) Temptations

Rev "T" the 3rd was anxious to be with the saints. He drove through the neighbourhood with high expectation. The sun was out, the birds were singing and Sister "V" wore her special brooch featuring her affection for her Lord and King "Jesus." The turquoise heart-shaped sculptured piece was given to her by her Grandfather just before his death.

Sister "V" chose to dress in a pastel twin-shaded dress and flowing hemline to accentuate her hips. Wearing high heels strengthen by a Velcro strapping; she walked with confidence and grace on the sidewalk. Her hair was up, supported and held in place with a long hair-pin that protruded out at a noticeable insatiable angle. Her husband was distracted when she walked in the living room. The Yves St Lauren perfume invaded his space and quickened his senses to stand to attention. He wanted her but she was on a different level of worship; to her husband dismay and disappointment.

The Feline retreated into the bushes and hid itself on a branch perched 9ft up in the tree. Felix the black cat had a panoramic view of the humanoids as they came out to worship. The adapted nocturnal eyes of Felix screened the inner corner and crevices of the Purley-Gate Pew, looking for the elusive creature who had caused his embarrassing eviction from his second home.

The Choir were seated when the Worship Leaders stood up to whisk up the mood of the Christian Worshippers. The guitar player slapped the strings in tandem with the drummer; sending a sonic booming effect throughout the building. The people rocked and swayed from side to side as the tambourines banged and rattled to the beat. Spendeasy in his element demonstrated the ability to do the moonwalk on the parquet-floor. The moves caught the

Yielding (2) Temptations

imagination of the enthusiast as they changed their rhythm from being robotics geniuses to doing the Reggae-Skank in groups of four.

Sister "V" was too sophisticated to be involved with such frivolity. She always considered that moderation was needed at all times when dancing was involved in church services. She loved to dance but in appropriation of the event or environment. The rhythm and base from the music demanded a response and due respect; it was too good not to. "V" eventually stepped out in the isle and lifted her hands to heaven and moved rhythmically with grace and style. Gyrating her hips slowly with every second beat to the slap-stringing guitarist, she was in her spiritual motional groove of praise and worship. She lost herself momentarily while in the Hallelujah phase of adoration to her God.

All the available Bachelors in the congregation stopped Skanking and were almost motionless at the sight of a virtuous woman in full spiritual flight. Rev "T" the 3rd was captured! Like a thief in the night caught on camera; he had tasted the forbidden ice-cream his mother warned him not to touch; he mentally licked and devoured the soft-smooth delight of his hearts desire, even if it meant punishment that could end in pain. He decided it was worth it, angling his head at 35 degrees he had to stop singing and wonder…and admire this work of fine art.

Elder Standford in tune with the beat was rigid with his upper body. He cornered the market for awareness, knowing exactly where he was at any given time. Not putting a foot out of place, he glided his nimble feet across the floor with pace and complexity rarely seen by a semi-elderly man. The Elder

Yielding (2) Temptations

was in his heights. The music now raise to a higher tempo, thwarted an avalanche of worshippers to move to the next level....

The Professor was rocked by a category 5 hurricane as Sister Alfonteen made her move to join her man on the dance floor. Alfonteen's speciality was the calypso with an attitude, dodging all the obstacles of spectators; she reached the Elder who was finishing his piece of the James Brown trade mark shuffle. Sister Alfonteen immediately got in the groove and held Elders hand while feeling the motions of the oceanic music. This was The Elders weakness, beginning the tempo of the reggae version of "Higher Higher"; he dropped the Thunder-Clapp move that was too challenging even for the youth.

Felix confused and outcast in his current predicament, was straining to view the action in the crevice and corners of the church floor. The undulating flow of the rhythm and base defocused his ability to be observant and hence retreated back to a crouched position awaiting confirmation of his luncheon meat.

Sister Chastity burst unto the platform with Run-Tings and took over the mike from the Worship Team. The church was on fire, the words of the song were now in-audible while the current of the music resonated like a Mexican wave, dozens of souls searcher and worshippers clambered to the front as Rev "T" summoned up all of his concentration to lay hands on the few souls requiring spiritual assistance.

Sister Alfonteen's duet dance in public created the obsession juice cocktail she craved and desired before the melting of her ice. The lemon effect had

Yielding (2) Temptations

vanished and a sweet aftertaste of accomplishment with the refilling of passion from the nimble Elder; sent shrills of fireballs through her aching body.

The Elder regained full consciousness and realised Sister Alfonteen was working up his spiritual appetite for more worship and...

He Stopped and laid his hands on her shoulder to catch her attention. The current of the music still flowed to a whispering tone. Sister Alfonteen now on cloud-nine of her man collapsed into his arms without restraint. The Elder positioned himself just in time to handle her with respect and integrity. The Bachelor boys still in recovery mode from Sister "V" hadn't noticed the need to help the Elder in distress; he carried her to a seat, to the annoyance of the disgruntled occupier. The Elder was confused and realised at that point he was the focus of the Council Board Members, Primarily Deacon Gamble. He had to think fast and act with decisiveness.

"RED ALERT" "RED ALERT". Felix spotted his lunch, lurking in the corner of his second home. Felix jumps down and dashes through…

Deacon Gamble approached the unauthorised seated Sister and Officers Board Executive Member-Elder Standford. The Elder stood up to greet his fellow officer, only to be summoned in public, to the office at the back of the church. Elder Standford glanced at Sister Alfonteen while avoiding the displeased eye of the once occupying seat member.

Somehow; without being seen, Felix was within striking distance of the rat,

Yielding (2) Temptations

when the drummer spotted the vermin; the scene slowed down like in the motion picture "The Matrix". The drummer yelled and the efficient slap-stringer guitarist scampered unto his chair for refuge. The Rhythm and Base was over and the focus of attention was the electrified looking black cat and the vermin holding unto the scrap of food obtained some moments earlier from the Pastor Fischer's Bin.

The Rat was cornered, instead of waiting for imminent capture and inevitable death; it manoeuvred its Rear legs in preparation for a burst of accelerated speed. Despite the humanoids coming ever closer with an intention to maim, the Rat decided it was going to run for it or die-trying! Shifting its eyes from left to right frantically surveying the decreasing space available; he thrust forward breaking the rat dung speed endurance record of 0-10 droppings in 5 seconds.

Sister Alfonteen aroused by the commotion in the pew jump on her feet, de-stabilising the evicted visitor, she lifted her feet instinctively as Elder Standford came to the rescue. Elder Standford now in reverse motion and disobeying orders encased Sister Alfonteen in his arms to avoid the stricken rat on a desperate run. Sister Alfonteen arms embraced her knight in shinning armour as he circled around in search of a clear path to unburden his heavily laden arms.

The young men challenged with capturing the rat encroached with pace with an intention to kill. The men adjusted themselves as the approaching rat was trying to break away. The brothers lunged forward in unison like an American Football team dashing for the important Touchdown. The rat dislodged its

Yielding (2) Temptations

bruised Vermin legs and headed for the church entrance. Felix capturing live coverage of the failed imprisoned attempt, sprung into action with his appetite that was without a doubt turning into insatiable yearning for meat. The Carnivorousness of Felix was out of control. The need to eat this particular meat was beyond feline expression. Only action with complete satisfaction could pacify his hunger and thirst for food. Sister Alfonteen screamed out "Jesus Help Me" Elder Stanford replied "He already has." With this comforting assurance she wilted in his arms and drifted away while Elder Stanford staggered with discomfort to release the burden of a heavy woman.

Pastor Fischer regretting every moment of the deception, slid into a psychological recession. The thought of losing all the opportunities of life without a fighting chance, snared the ability to feel positive about the future. The loss of his Church, His Lover, His Wife, His Brethren and Friends and including his Family, brought about tears and an excruciating abdominal pain that could never be filled with calories.

Sunday morning arrived when Pastor Fischer was taken to the Truth Drug Test Room. Not conscious of the day of the week, the frightened specimen for truth testing was not ready emotionally for what was to come. The Scientist's in white suits motioned for action as the English unsuspecting patient was laid like a battering ram prepared for mind slaughter. Needles and Pins arrayed with perfect precision were laid out in advance ready for the proffessional mind invader. Pastor Fischer felt a sharp pain in his arms as they released his straight jacket for the first time for several hours. The shoulders being tense with muscle dysfunction unsettled the scientist trying to strap him into another contraption. Pastor Fischer used the convulsion tactics again to buy

Yielding (2) Temptations

him some time. Randomly convulsing and jerking spasmodically while releasing yellow spittle from the corner of his mouth. From the corner of his eye, a woman in high heels stepped forward and produced a sterile piece of white cloth and gently wiped the excess phlegm from his mouth. The Pastor new at this point there was no point in continuing; this in mind he relaxed his limbs and closed his eyes.

The scientist motioned to each other for the process to begin. The Serum causing a control of the patient cognitive behaviour was inserted into the arm. A last shudder in defiance was quickly abated within a few seconds of the Serum taking effect. Pastor Fischer was now under the complete control of the scientist.

Pastor Fischer aroused by frantic activity in the makeshift theatre; sensed a breakthrough for the scientist. Men and women in white coats wearing immaculate shoes scurried and screeched along the white buffed polished floor. A machine indicator behind the English Patient sounded with a high tone, as two extremely efficient looking doctors released their stethoscopes from around there necks to examine the Bishops condition. Something was wrong! One of them said. He tried to speak but the words uttered were delivered with a slur. He had no control of his left jaw and tongue, with an irregular heartbeat it seemed like the curtains were being drawn on his life.. He could see his own heartbeat rise and fall on his chest, then a loud noise interrupted his panic driven concerns and he lost consciousness.

Yielding (2) Temptations

The scientist pulled out the once hidden defibrillation machine to revive the irregular heartbeat of the Bishop. Bodies of Doctors and Nurses burst through into the room to aid the sometimes possibly catastrophic after-effect of the Truth drug.

Sister "V" still hypnotized by being on a spiritual high without the melody, came to her senses as the scene before her was not considered normal. The once Rock my Soul Slap Stick guitarist who played with such fervent spiritual enthusiasm; was shaking with irrational fear of something around him. Sister "V" motioned common sense to the situation. Piecing together the action of the guitarist, church young men scoring zero on failed touchdowns and watching Elder Stanford; in whom she held a high regard, was spinning around with Sister Alfonteen as she was being whisked away in his arms with a smile on her face.

Then she saw it. The Beast! As a child back home in the West Indies, Sister V was used to catching green lizards. She would after school search and destroy all invading reptilian that crossed the path of her home. Her parents encouraged this attitude to unwanted creatures and rewarded her efforts by giving extra pocket money as a reward for each capture. The same instincts to search and destroy were aroused in her now.

She noticed the fire extinguisher filled with carbon dioxide Co_2, hinged on the bracket close to the church entrance. She dashed forward passing Elder Standford performing a premature manoeuvre in carrying the bride across the threshold. Felix approaching from behind Sister "V" was unaware of the danger. "V" positioned the fire extinguisher and aimed it at the oncoming Rat. The rat changed direction to avoid a collision but her youthful and instinctive

Yielding (2) Temptations

reaction came to fruition. The Rat had no chance. The white smoke was clearing as Felix was mesmerised with perplexity. The young men who failed to score looked on with amazement as Rev "T" the 3rd released the nozzle handle from sister "V".

The whole congregation was stunned as Sister "V" unconcerned with everyone's reaction, approached the Ice-landic Rat, now deep frozen for eminent removal. Taking a white tissue from the pocket of Rev "T" she stooped down and lifted the once living vermin and carried it outside and disposed of it in the commercial dustbin.

She turned around to face the church music. Everybody clapped and applauded the courage of Sister "V". Elder Standford still carrying his bride across the threshold came face to face with Deacon Gamble. The Deacon acknowledged the accomplishment of sister "V" with a half nod and smile as he stood still in front of The Elder. Tapping his feet the Elder lowered and released his acting bride with the help of sister "V" and followed the Deacon into the back room for an immediate dressing down.

Yielding (2) Temptations

Y (2) T

Scene 8

The newborns kittens wondering in the backyard of the Grangers residence began to feel the winter chill blistering on their reddened cheeks; as the little felines scampered back inside of their sheltered housing, their little legs shivered and trembled on contact with the ground. The pond now frozen over with a thin layer of ice was advantageous for bird skating. Dozens of birds flew down at speed and applied the wing-motion wing-brake to cause a skid on the ice-runway. The bird activists pecked their way through the ice to capture food they once enjoyed in the autumn months; understanding the environmental science was never strong among birds. The Grangers loved their little kittens and seeing their plight ushered them into the house while wrapping the weakest link with a blanket.

The curtains were closing fast on the fast Becoming – "late Pastor Fischer". He hung unto life by a thread, the doctors screamed out to the assistants for help to resuscitate the dying Bishop waiting on death-row. The Pastor's fleeting moments of precious life began to ebb away as his finger tips and lips started to change to a darker shade. More effort was required to overturn the dismal cards of death. The Grim Reaper signalled that it was time for the Pastor to accompany him on his travels, but fate had a different plan…

Rev "T" the 3rd finally reached the moment to deliver the awe inspiring sermon. The commotion earlier had caused a distraction that had stemmed the

Yielding (2) Temptations

flow of the Spirit of the believers. The Batchelor Brothers still mystified and confused, appreciated the talent and bravery of a Sister they had admired in praise and worship. Elder Standford stood accused before Deacon Gamble of inappropriate behaviour with Sister Alfonteen. The sentence was banishment for an undisclosed period. He never felt so alone, desperate and in need of encouragement. He looked to Rev "T" the 3rd for inspiration. The Slap String guitarist regained his composure after the emotional set-back and played with gusto and affirmation. Rev "T" was ready, the congregation was ready, and now the moment was right to perform his grand finale.

The congregation knelt down as Deacon Gamble prayed for the anointing to be upon the Minister. The Deacon laid his hands on the shoulder of the young Preacher as Sister Chastity moved to the front. After the prayer, Sister Chastity felt compelled to approach the man of God to deliver a personal instruction from the Lord in the ear of the Ministering Servant.

Rev "T" the third caught the eye of Sister Chastity as she delivered this instruction, You must be pure, your heart must be clean and your vessel must be washed with the pure water of sanctification before the blessing can take true effect on the congregation you are to serve." The Rev was confused and the message he was to deliver moments later was lost, his confidence and enthusiasm to preach his life changing message was now dashed. He knew the message was sent from on High.

After the message was delivered, Pastor "T" opened the sacred Hymns and Solos song-book for an immediate inspiration and comfort to his desperate soul. A message had to be delivered, but what message. He was confused and

Yielding (2) Temptations

bewildered to what this message would be. The time for a special divine inspiration was needed with an instant effect. The Worship Leaders were performing to their best, the congregation stood on their feet giving special thanks to God for his Mercy and Grace. As the song his "Grace and Mercy" penetrated through the crowd, many hands were lifted up to god, and a Hallelujah praise was initiated with intent and purpose .

Rev "T" the 3rd mustered up some courage in the light of his impending predicament. The power of the Holy Spirit had to take control of the situation quickly. The Reverend was drawing himself into a deeper and deeper hole. He stepped forward to be the man of the Hour, the first real message of his life the people would take seriously and remember for a very long time. The people position their attention to the Minister to receive what was dually expected to be an inspiriting and emotional and spiritual speech with passion and sterility of truth. The Reverend for the very first time in years was afraid of standing in the gap to deliver the message of the hour. As he approach the congregation. Tears of humility and helplessness overcame his feeble-minded soul. The Church was moved with compassion and respect. They knew this was a momentous day for this young inspiring Minister. He was highly respected by the Ministers Council, loved by the Youth and adored by some of the Single Minded Sisters. His shoulder bore the burdens of past sins and ungodly activities. He cried internally asking for deliverance and to allow God to use him expeditiously without restraint; to let God's will be done on earth as it is in Heaven and allow the Daily Bread of the Word Of God to Penetrate the hearts of the believers waiting to blessed.

A faint sound of hope was triggered when the Defibrillator function power

Yielding (2) Temptations

setting was on maximum. The professional's hair stood on end as they cleared the area as the patient shock treatment was coming to a successful end, delight and joy filled the room with applause from the medical staff as the patient's heart monitor returned to an almost normal pattern. Pastor Fischer tongue still numb from the after-effects began to recover consciousness. Swirling his head from side to side in hope of shaking off the awkward feeling of unrecovered limbs, Pastor tried to lift his hands, still strapped to the table for protection the doctors felt it was appropriate to release him for little while to aid the recovery process.

The Pastor still groggy from the Truth Drug started to ask questions in words barely legible for dialogue. "Gwat gav you dun to me? Why cant I feeeeel my arrrrrm ? Gwat gav you dun too meeee? The Doctors crowded around the patient, watching and trying to understand the words he was struggling to convey. An unusual looking mind with one-eye and a black patch stepped forward. He was clearly the chief Consultant. Whipping out his stethoscope he recorded his breathing and stress level. Taking careful notes from the Heart monitoring machine he called the other Doctors in the far corner of the room and began to whisper, what seemed to be instructions. All the Doctors turned around while nodding their heads in unison. A gentleman's agreement was reached when the one-eyed Doctor left the room in hast.

The Nurse was informed of the new instructions from the general Doctors. The Patient had to be sedated another time due to the risk of brain damage. Pastor Fischer was recovering fast. His eyes now wide open and his mind alert to everything that was happening in the room. The nurse felt no empathy with the patient, she kept a professional distance between him and made no

Yielding (2) Temptations

unnecessary comments and portrayed no feeling for this Patient.

Pastor Fischer coming to terms with life again with a dead tongue appreciated the opportunities to right the wrong committed to individuals in his life. He decided it was time to tell the truth no matter what it would cost him, even if this would cost him his life. He felt it was worth it, just to see his family one-more time.

His eyes was closing again and he had no control. With the dead tongue; he tried to explain the need to stay awake and not to sleep, vowing to speak the truth the whole truth and nothing but the truth.

The Doctors were satisfied the truth Drug was working as expected. The patient was willing to tell them everything they needed to know but his deteriorating condition prevented him from taking the appropriate action. All the signs were good before the effects began to emerge. The patient was responding to the drug and the information about his history started to flow. They were encourage with all the signs. Then, out of nowhere, he stopped talking as if he knew he was been taped in his unconscious state. The Doctors were baffled as to how he could have known. No known cases in military history had ever happened like Pastor Fischer's, he is the only person in history to react to Serum in a negative fashion. The patients dose was checked and rechecked several times over the period to ensure the correct amount had been applied. The Doctors were sure that was no mistake had taken place.

Sister Alfonteen still transfixed from her cocktails of lemon and lime -Standford Juice, tried her very best to control the emotions through the

Yielding (2) Temptations

important sermon of Rev "T" the 3rd. The people responded positively to the earnest plea of the Preacher. The tears of genuine passion from his words was felt from the smallest to the more mature individual members of the church. Sister Alfonteen delighted by the action of her saviour,. Felt comforted and loved by her Pro-Minted Knight in the Shining Armour. The taste of memory cocktails filled her mind and body with everlasting memories for a lifetime. The moment her man had taken charge of the situation without batting an eyelid, nourished her desires for more sequential affection. The desired Champagne cork had been popped and the froth was bubbling over her loving passionate soul.

The Preacher cried with tears of uncertainty mixed with passion of fervency. The need to place your all at the alter never came at a better time. The people flowed with the spirit of the preacher, captivating the meaningfulness of the moment to seek God with due diligence and urgency. Rev "T" inhibition was thrown away,. The undiluted backing of the Holy Spirit came with confirmation through the Amen and praises. The Revered coursed through the scripture like a professional seasoned with the word. The organist measured timing on the build-up of the Preachers punch-lines emphasised his points. The resonated sounds of applause and nodding of heads confirmed the new Reverend standing in his new confirmed ministry.

Elder Standford entangled in a web of fanaticism and uncontrollable spiritual behaviour, sat stoned face while Rev "T's" passionate plea for genuine worship and honesty was aired on the pew. Elder Standford face said it all, treated as a commoner from Deacon Gamble and told to sit at the back of the church while being observed closely by his colleagues, clearly was a

Yielding (2) Temptations

intimidatory tactic to shame in open church a once respected member of the council.

The Elder felt he had lost control of the situation when Sister Alfonteen had exposed the weakness he thought would never be viewed by all and sundry. For years he had taken pride in himself with self discipline and self control of difficult circumstances. The moment Deacon Gamble had called him in public, humiliation had set in and depression got a hold of his spirit. Listening to the Preacher didn't help in any way; his mind was too far away to comprehend the implication of the action statements of the Preacher. The possibility of the Brothers talking about him behind his back and smearing his good name he had lived to protect with so much vigour; was at stake. Too much effort and endless energy was invested in his character. The thought of gossipers broadcasting his name on the BT-Line-Gazette open frequency channel; sent a feeling of anger and resentment coursing through his veins.

Rev "T" the 3rd motioned the Power of the Holy Spirit to purge the souls that sinned against God and Man. He welcome the chance for the guilty parties to make peace with their enemies. He quoted "Now is the acceptable time of the Lord, come to the alter and make your peace with Man and then with God". A Chorus was sung to lighten the load for people to congregate to make amends. He invited everyone to greet each other and to encourage the faint-hearted to make the first move in asking for forgiveness. Many woman and men greeted each other warmly, others had tears in their eyes while embracing a once distant now close friends. The Spirit of forgiveness swept the place as the people started to feel a real sense of release in the place. The Reverend swung his gown-trail to one side as he welcomed the free spirited souls that released

Yielding (2) Temptations

the tension of malice they once endured.

Reverend felt his mission was almost accomplished when Sister "V" was ministering to a young woman in need. This obviously was a moment two women needed to share the inner feelings of broken hearts. The young woman in black was beautiful and well proportioned in all features. The Reverend had to take a second look at her stunning features that had caught the eyes of the many unexpected married men. Sister "V" held her left arm, and providing a shouldering support with meaningful words of wisdom, which obviously reached the soul. The young woman started to cry effortlessly as she lifted her arms in the air and said Lord hear me and forgive me in this time of greatest need. You know my trial and the pains I am going through at this moment, I am depending on you to release me from the situation I am not in control of. Whatever happened to my… and then she opened her eyes, realising that she was being watched. Sister "V" encouraged her to let it out and let yourself go. The woman in Black instantly changed her line of prayer and asked for more strength to overcome her current trials and tribulation.

Sister Chastity was suddenly on fire, she obviously received a word from the Lord with Brimstone. She marched to the front of the crowd with ferocity and fire. Spewing out damnation to the unknown person; who she predicted was asking God for forgiveness while being guilty of a heinous crime of intent. Sister Chastity encircled a group of people including the mystery woman, while stomping her feet in annoyance. She began to speak in tongues as the church went silent. They expected and interpreter to intervene and give a interpretation to the individual concerned. The room was quiet as the wind brushing through the trees outside was heard. The music paused in bated

Yielding (2) Temptations

breath from a Word from God. Heads were bowed in respect to the messenger who would be chosen to deliver the all important message. Sister Chastity stayed silent as it was not her turn to broadcast the answer to the riddle of the tongues.

A little girl aged seven stepped forward. Sophia was a special instrument with ministerial qualities of distinction. Her mother and father died in a car crash when she was only 12-months old. Her Grandmother, known as Ina, had taken the responsibility to look after the child. She loved and cared for her in a special way. Bringing her up in the way of the Lord; she imparted wisdom and extra tuition about life and culture in her early stage of her life. Sophia absorbed all the information and added her own reasoning to the areas Ina left out; still only seven years old, she had an intelligence of an older woman.

She closed her eyes and seemed to float into space. Her voice carried far and wide into every corner of the church, it resonated through the congregation with decibels ringing in every ear. She delivered the word from the throne of God.

"God is not pleased my Brethren, you come to be blessed but your heart is far from him. Cleanse your heart and purify your minds from the sins of this world that you have committed. Confession is needed if your prayers are to be answered." She opened her eyes and beheld the lady in black. Reverend "T" trembling for fear; he started to piece together the puzzle that later was to have an impact on every church member from this day on. Sister Chastity clasped her hands together knowing the next message was going to be a warning. The kind of warning, if ignored, life might be forever lost. The little girl came face

Yielding (2) Temptations

to face with the lady in black and held out her finger and pointed to her stomach. She said abomination, abomination, what you have in there is an abomination. The lady in black was already embarrassed but with the stressing of the fact from a little innocent Prophetess that she was pregnant was too much. She shook her head with wild eyes and confrontational lips of desperate ineptitude. This was her lowest and most vulnerable, moment. A little child exposing her nakedness and shame in front of the entire congregation. And then forging ahead with the prophecy to give the name of the unborn babies father, Pastor Fischer.

The little girl retreated back to her seat while glancing back at the woman in black with distain. The woman in black blushed. She was desperate to say something that would discredit the little Prophetess, but couldn't find anything to say, she couldn't deny that she was pregnant and the evidence was beginning to show. The Lady in black slumped into the arms of Sister "V", who also was piecing together the pieces with Reverend "T". The room was still quite and tense, everybody's eyes was involved in a conversation with each other through telepathy. The writing was on the wall, the new revelation was out and the gossiper had sufficient meat to feast on. The Lady in Black was ushered to her seat as Rev "T" the 3rd clearly shaken and stirred; he attempted to finish the service on a positive note. Whispers from around the church were evidently featuring the headliner "Lady in Black" as many heads turned around together when the new gossip was translated to the people who hadn't heard Sophie had spoken those infamous words of condemnation.

Sister Chastity summoned a meeting with her crew. A new topic to be dissected.

Yielding (2) Temptations

Sister Chastity and Run-Tings hotly debated the revelation of the Lady in Black. Questions arose with the possible link between Pastor Fischer and the unborn child, Sister Chastity felt compelled to probe the history of the said woman. How could they prove this was Pastor Fischer child and what appropriate steps could be taken in the Pastors absence. Run-Tings paced the room and began to pray. He felt uneasy with all the speculation even though the thought of his Pastor cavorting with a single woman repulsed his spirit.

While the evening droned on, sister V's telephone line buzzed without a pause. She knew the drill and the women in the church were on the war path to establish the visual confirmation from a person that saw it all happen. This time she was not going to be a willing party. Tears of fearful emotion for Pastor Fischer and the unborn child toiled in her mind. The Woman in Black was very beautiful she thought, but how could Pastor!, My Pastor! Do such a thing, stooping so low behind Sister Fischer's back to have an affair and ultimately a child. Was he planning to leave Sister Fischer and the church defenceless with this scandal? I think not! "V" said to herself. The shock was too great, after the service; "V" had to ask the Lady in Black for her address details. She guessed she wouldn't have given it unless it was asked for. Sister "V" husband, Burt, had arrived home after drinking heavily at the pub. He took one look at his wife to establish her mood, she shuffled to one side in disapproval of his condition and he walk away into the kitchen to fix himself a sobering spiritless drink.

Pastor "T" the 3rd accomplished the preaching mission with relative success but his moment was robbed by the revelation of the young Prophetess.

Yielding (2) Temptations

Run-Tings called his mobile to congratulate him on a job well done. The second phase of his call was all about the Woman in Black. Nobody knew her name. The Reverend found it strange nobody knew her and worse still, nobody knew if she would ever return. Run-Ting said that he had prayed about it and he will leave everything to God and Sister Chastity. Reverend "T" the 3rd thought it wise to warn Run-Tings that, many things have been said behind Pastor Fischer back and suggested an element of cautioned would be required when discussing this matter with any member of the church. Run-Tings had to bite his lip and agree.

Bishop Fisher was coming around. Doctors looked in earnest for signs of his returning to normal health. Monitors and tubes positioned in every orifice and blood pressure points. His heart, lungs, Liver pancreas was under inspection for any abnormality. All the signs seemed to be good. They proceeded with the check list, ensuring that no mistakes were made. They identified the problem earlier with the dosage, the Junior Doctor who had administered the dosage used the wrong measuring device for the quantity of the Serum to be administered. He was immediately dismissed even though the Consultant should have checked it himself but decided a scapegoat was needed to cover his own mistake. Pastor Fischer's sensory organs were back to normal operation, his tongue and left arm reacted perfectly to his will and command. He felt a sense of relief when the nurse came to him and ask if he felt better. He courteously replied, "much better, so much better". The nurse filled out a form while taking the reading from the paper trail monitors, then left the room.

Pastor Fischer thought about his last moments when he promised God to

Yielding (2) Temptations

reveal all and to be honest about his extra-marital affairs. He knew the implication and the sentence that it would carry. He decided it was time to give up on the Woman he loved and go back to his wife to start all over again on a clean slate. Not knowing the condition of his wife gave doubt in his mind if he would ever have the chance to make amends but he would certainly try. He became insistent in his mind not to disclose his affair to anyone first apart from his wife.. How he was going to achieve it would be his challenge. First he must devise a plan to get himself released, he had tried this before unsuccessfully but this time he had Ace-Card to play with. His life had been put at risk because of a professionals negligence, he was held prisoner against his will and without reason, and not proven to be a threat to National Security. He had all the reason and even though his reason for release was valid, it was going to take something very special to make it happen.

His last memory he had of his wife as she was carried down the stair to the awaiting ambulance, deepened his conviction to see her again, to help put a smile back on her face and to live up to the standard the brethren came to expect from their leader. Pastor Fischer had let himself down; submitting to temptation of the world without a fight was no-way for a Preacher to behave. Making amends now would cement his relationship with God and gain the respect from the church, and feel positive about himself as a man of God. The gauntlet needed to be thrown down and the task needed to be done. The only obstacle in his way was His lover, and the Military. How he needed to achieve these goals needed careful planning and meticulous timing.

Ina had an unexpected visitor at her home, Sophia hiding around the corner of

Yielding (2) Temptations

the kitchen was weary of trouble that might be caused due to the Sunday morning service, she listened very carefully to Sister Chastity and Run-Tings as they felt the need to pray and discuss the morning issues surrounding the Sunday morning. Sister Chastity did not seem very pleased with Ina, stating her concerns on a child warning a grown woman about personal matters. Sister Chastity understood the importance of the message and the authenticity, however, she felt Sophia needed guidance on the subject of appropriateness. Ina insisted the Lord was in control of the situation and Sophia was only an instrument of the Lord. Run-Tings felt compelled to interject with his views. Run-Tings accepted the gift of the young girl, this issue Run-Ting said was not questionable. He proceeded with his concerns on the church ladies being very upset on the embarrassment of the Lady in Black. Ina defended her Granddaughter; if there are any questions that needed to be answered you must ask the Lord and not ask Sophia to address a message sent from Heaven, Even though she appreciated Sister Chastity and Run-Tings, she felt the matter was in the Lords hands and nobody else.

Sister Chastity felt Ina was to liberal with the facts and should have at least looked into the issue with a little more sensitivity to the ladies cause. Ina insisted again, this is not and was not necessary; the Lord is in control and if this message in words and deeds were challenged in any way by anyone, she would leave such a person to the creator to deal with and warned! Touch Not the Lord's Anointed.

Ina felt pressured by Sister Chastity by her presence. The sole reason for her visit was not to encourage the gift, God had bestowed on such a young child but to bring her down. This level of disparagement would have to be

Yielding (2) Temptations

discouraged. Ina's strength came from her conviction as a Grandmother and a Parent. Losing her two dearest darling children in a car crash only a few years ago was devastating. She vowed to God and the Child, that nobody as long as she has any breath would take advantage of this child. Ina valued the gift in Sophia and encouraged openness in her ministry to preach the gospel according to the leading of the Holy Spirit.

After the unwanted visitors left, Sophia went to her Grandmother for encouragement on the matter. Ina cuddled little Sophia in love, assured Sophia of her full support. Even though Sophia was a young prophetess she still required the support of her family. She was still very tender and vulnerable and easily distracted from the objectiveness of the message God bestowed on her. Ina was proud of her little princess, her only pride and joy she has left in life after such a tragedy of the past. Her only son dealing crack cocaine on the east coast in the United States, raised her blood pressure to a dangerous level and an unhealthy feeling of under-achievement in family overwhelmed her passionate soul. Ina needed to set the record straight and get things right again. The chance to accomplish something she failed earlier on in her life and all this energy to be channelled through this one child; Sophia! Ina decided it was time to pray and ask god to protect his servant. She knew from common knowledge the Brethren in the church would do absolutely everything to undermine the movement of God through this little child. Ina was intent on succeeding in all her expectation and confronted anyone who would dare criticize God's choice of a servant

Sister Chastity still seething from her previous encounter encouraged Run-Tings to help her pray. She felt that Ina could have at least talked to her

Yielding (2) Temptations

daughter rather than shame an innocent woman with an embarrassing message. Run-Tings kept quiet knowing if he committed himself into this discussion, he would have to pay the consequence. Run-Tings understood Sister Chastity. Once; strong feeling emerged on the surface from nowhere which Sister Chastity tuned into. A Self declaration that they were human highlighted the fact. they embraced each other in a momentary phase of celebration; when good news swept the close friends in Christ.

Sister Chastity loved his masterful way of dealing with awkward circumstances and his wisdom which when in character demonstrates the manliness she craved in the man. He knows her weak spot and even though Run-Tings was completely unaware, she never failed to go weak at the knees just listening to his sense of reasoning.

Run-Tings sensed the moment to bring Sister Chastity back into line, he knew it would be tricky, treading very carefully on Sister Chastity emotions and finding the right moment to unleash his wisdom, he sense for the first time in their encounter, Sister Chastitys willingness to welcome an intervention and he was not in the mood to disappoint her. He initiated a mental prayer with a slight glance to heaven for spiritual guidance.

Run-Tings cleared his throat and his deep authoritive voice sprung to life. "Sister Chastity, it is a commonly well known fact that God decides what is deemed appropriate and what is inappropriate in all circumstance. Understanding that God chose a little girl must indeed be symbolic and purposeful for the recipient. The Lady in Black receiving a message even though it was in the open, will have had the desired effect for the message to

Yielding (2) Temptations

be most potent. I think it is unwise for any of us to interfere with the working of God. Sister Chastity, like a little girl chastised, recognised the importance of Run-Tings words and submitted herself to his reasoning and both agreed to pray about the matter.

While Ina was on her knees praying, her spirit quickened. A sense of God creating a solution to her concerns seemed imminent. She raised her hands to heaven and thanked the God of Heaven for answering her prayers by faith.

Elder Standford felt compelled to release his anger, the frustration, the pain and anguish he felt when Deacon Gamble called him out in the open, compounded the need to take revenge on a solid object, this object was his faithful and beloved car. A dent appeared after a hefty kick on the door was initiated with his uncontrolled emotion. The Elder pounced on his lawn with displeasure while trying to salvage some dignity while the neighbours looked on with worried expressions. The Elder sat down in his recliner chair trying to piece everything together on what had happened. How he could have been so foolish and foolhardy, he said to himself. It's all Sister Alfonteen's fault for preying on his weak spot. He felt this was the perfect time to re-align his principals into some affirmative action. He vowed no woman would be in a position to manoeuvre their intention with effect without his due process of approval. Sister Alfonteen became his new nemesis, how he was going to deal with this sensually infectious woman, was certainly going to be a difficult challenge. The Elder began to click his fingers, something he habitually did when uncertain.

The afternoon loomed with the scent of freshly cut mayflowers displayed in

Yielding (2) Temptations

the Elders living room, the flowers naturally fragranced his quarters with the coolness of spring as the Elder struggled to find the answer he desperately needed. It was decision time, the Elder had to step up to the plate of his uncertainty and take control. He wanted Sister Alfonteen to stop her advances and desist from further encounters. How the Elder was going to achieve this demise would be difficult, due to the fact, very little knowledge was known of his adversary.

In a flash the Elder had got IT!

The answer was knowledge; He needed background information on the adversary. The kind of information, that first; would be incriminating and second, would be advantageous in using at a later stage. Obtaining this information was going to tricky, should he try the direct approach or should he do it discreetly by undercover informants? He pondered these questions through his mind, over and over again for many hours, searching for the perfect solution to his question.

The Woman in Black cursed and tossed her pillow with anger. How could a little girl reveal her inner secrets and undying love for the Shepherd of the flock, and also the revelation in unveiling her sins in her womb in the presence of the church that her lover belonged to? The young Usher "Spendeasy" had slipped her his number for contact on a makeshift church business card. A routine commonly practiced if it was known a visitor was too shy to provide their personal details. The Lady took the card out of her bag and slowly waved the card in the air, while contemplating her next move. After a moment She grabbed the phone and dialled his number with a vexated spirit. Flashbacks of

Yielding (2) Temptations

the events of the day revisited her mind, the little girl's eyes was piercing the guilty soul. Her pointed finger seemed larger than life while she contemplated the audiences response and reaction. Revealing the secret of her unborn child to the world was unforgivable. But what could she do? What in the world could she have said to this Prophetess child to justify a response? The Lady could not argue with an innocent child and she was too afraid to challenge the secret facts. If it was an adult that had spoken to her in the service then she would have had just cause to retaliate with venom. She accepted her fate, the secret was out and she knew the people would talk and gossip, but her feelings for her Lover was stronger than any so-called Christian's gossip. Her course was set, she needed to find her man and reveal to him her undying Love.

The Woman's Unauthorised Activist, manned the exchanged lines to discuss the pending pregnancy with the estrange Woman in Black. Sister Fox (AKA: Ina-You-Business) tried Sister "V" line to update herself and the Clan from a witness point of view. Sister Ina-You-Business relentlessly called her number for over an hour. She knew Sister "V" was home from a local informant of Sister "V"'s neighbour Mrs Mangul. She gave up after a while and adlibbed her stories using her gossip experience to add sugar and spice to the already hot debate.

Although the death of Sister Stray was still fresh in the minds and hearts of the congregation, they felt the blame should squarely be placed on the administration of the church assembly. With the news of Woman's Privacy being exposed by a child, they felt the same passion for the injustice served on the visitor. Sister Chastity received a call from Sister Ina-You-Business and was asked the important question that would dominate the proceedings to

Yielding (2) Temptations

follow. Sister Chastity who was still with Run-Tings, involved him in hearing the reasoning's of Sister Ina-You-Business.

Sister Ina-You-Business coughed meaningfully as to clear any obstacle in her airways. "Sister Ina-You Business being in this church for over thirty two years had delivered 3 babies for the ladies in the Youth Choir and contributed heavily to the Women's Ministry Building Fund; she felt eligible after Sister Stray, to continue the carrying of the mantel for fairness in the way women were being portrayed in the church." Ina-You-Business changed the positioning of her handset; now to her left ear. "Women need Protection and Encouragement not only from the Leaders of the Assembly but also from the congregation. What happened to this woman was a blatant act of aggression against a visitor from a child." Sister Chastity nudged Run-Tings for help. Ina-You-Business raised her voice while echoing down the line as the two listeners trembled in fear of what was coming. Ina-You-Business still waited for the previous question to be answered, although she offered no pause in her sentence, and went straight into the pledge of mandatory allegiance statement from Sister Chastity; she said, "which side are you on" Sister?

Sister Ina-you-Business was not prepared for niceties, a straight, strong affirmative answer was required to her question. Sister Stray died trying to convey the important message of loyalty and devotion for the ladies and Sister Ina-You-Business was ready for the unfinished challenge to be completed with success. Ina-You-Business was waiting to get on with business, with a frown on her brow, baited breath, and her fingers twitching in anticipation, she was waiting for her major campaign contributor Sister Chastity and her Group of the Prayer Ban warriors to join her crew of the disorderly ladies in

Yielding (2) Temptations

Christ.

Spendeasy took respite after the service. He pondered about the Woman in Black that caught his eye in the service. He knew Sophia from Sunday school and knowing well her dedication to the scriptures, came to the undisputed conclusion the message delivered was from the Lord. From experience, Speandeasy could only imagine what the young church Ladies would say about the unappropriateness of it all. He thought, could the Pastor really get a stranger, pregnant? Looking back in history he remembered the sermons and lectures Pastor Fischer made on the subject of infidelity. Spendeasy reviewed his notes the Pastor covered only a few weeks ago. Sunday: December 6th, MASTERING YOUR CARNAL AFFECTIONS THROUGH THE WORD!

2Co 10:4 (For the weapons of our warfare *are* not carnal, but are mighty through God to the pulling down of strong holds;)

Spendeasy's Notes: The world draws the mind into the earthly things of the flesh. A man must be transformed by the renewing of his mind. The mind is the key to the success of a Christian to overcome the flesh. The flesh when tempted and fails to ovcercome, becomes a strong hold and then becomes a mighty stronghold. Just like the Berlin Wall that kept the freedom of the citizens to roam from East to West, so is the Strong Hold that prevents a Christian from experiencing the freedom to explore righteousness in God. Warfare must be experienced in order to achieve the victory in battle in the spiritual realm.

Yielding (2) Temptations

To conquer feelings there must be a resistance to sin in the mind. The Body must subject itself to the mind and the will of God. To change the mind of man that is born in sin and shapen in iniquity, he must have Perseverance, Patience and Grace from God.

Gal 5:16 *this* I say then, Walk in the Spirit, and ye shall not fulfill the lust of the flesh.

Notes: The flesh will always war against the spirit and spirit against the flesh. This is the impediment of man and constant earthly battle of the inner man. A man knows what is right but the flesh desires to be pleased and teased with all the refinement and pleasure of the flesh. Reaching out to God in prayer and fasting must be subjected to the will of a man wanting the desire to reach God's perfection and will. This cannot be achieved through man's own will because sin is like an in-growing toe-nail that will push itself through the nail that is good, in doing so, it presents itself like a thorn in the side of a man that is travelling to a far country.

Putting off the old man with his deeds and trying to follow the Lord's Commandments, comes with a price. The flesh will cry out for satisfaction and the Spirit will soothe the aching heart of the wandering pilgrim that desire to do evil. To be Spiritually minded involves searching and mentally absorbing the scriptures with due-diligence and faith. Believing the lord to accomplish any task in removing the mountains that is in the way of the Believer, will help a sinner who is trying to fulfil the scripture in its entirety succeed.

Yielding (2) Temptations

Spendeasy turned the page and looked to the Heavens for inspiration. How Pastor Fischer could preach such hope and glory and delivered with vigorous theological soundness, while committing sin, was beyond him. Spendeasy shook his head in bewilderment, then, the phone rang.

Yielding (2) Temptations

Y (2) T

Scene 9

Elder Standford decided it was time for revenge. Placing emphasis on his current mental state, the forum had to be set to put in place an order of eviction. Nothing was going to survive the onslaught he was about to unleash. Cries for mercy would ring out. The unrelenting and merciless conduit of his intention was being made ready to clean sweep every corner of the offenders solitary home. The Elder stood poised to start his pursuit. With Sister Alfonteen firmly on his mind, an innocent life was about to be lost with a curtailed smile on his face. His broom was firm and ready, the cockroaches saw their doom. The nest would be violently shaken with Anti-Cockroach Spray. Life was indeed about to be lost, Standford was about to avenge his fury with a momentary feeling of satisfaction. The process had begun and the Cockroaches scrambled in every direction of the basement for refuge and a hiding place. Standford had covered all his areas well. The cockroach was outmatched, outsmarted and outmanoeuvred in every sense of the word.

Battle lines were erected, as the first wave of the refugee cockroaches died without gaining any significant victories. When the broom swept heavily in the corners, many cockroaches got caught up within the bristles. Elder Standford also got this under control. A bowl of steaming hot water was at the doorway for this very purpose. The Elder dipped the hiding refugees into hot

Yielding (2) Temptations

grave of the once thriving Roach Tavern. To add insult to injury, he sprayed the bristles with the Anti-cockroach spray which snuffed the life of their already suffocating airways. The sound of the scampering feet of the insect kingdom multiplied. The walls now revealing the true level of infestation of cockroaches, signalled the time for the mass extermination. A machine he hired from the exterminator was draped over his shoulder. This was going to be a quick and painful death, with his face mask clearly secured; the terminator pointed the killing machine at the unwelcomed squatters. Instinctively they sensed more danger and changed direction when the trigger was pressed. Elder Standford found pleasure as the infestation was quickly coming to an abrupt end. German Cockroaches falling in great numbers Elder Standford stood victorious in the battle against the unwanted insects. Bodies lying motionless on the battlefield, the twitching of legs featured the desperation and fight for life of the little creatures. A Male and Female German cockroach escaped. They both glanced back at their dead children. Frightened and nervous, they waited for the area to be free of danger. It would take months to replace all the dead comrades scattered all over the scene. Every cockroach had a name with a personality, this could never be replaced, and although life was short George and Gertrude felt compelled to soldier on this journey of survival.

Elder Standford surveyed his magnificent accomplishment. The dead visitors lay motionless as he watched the last breath of life, ebb away. He thought of Sister Alfonteen and her wretched selfish ways. How was he going to carry out his terminator's mentality on this sexual beast? Something like a smoking gun that would flush out all the impurities and secret sins of the past for him to expose in public for ridicule would do the trick. Standford derived inspiration

Yielding (2) Temptations

from his brief encounters with the unwanted visitors. It spurred on his drive to overcome all the obstacles that were in his way. Sister Alfonteen was not going to win. The Elder questioned within himself; why now, why is she targeting him now with such ferocity? Did he miss something? Was there a situation that kickstarted her emotions causing them to go into overdrive? So many unanswered questions, in order for him to come to any conclusion about the matter, he must first identify where the signals came from.

Cunning as a serpent, Elder Standford decided it was time to polly-fill the gaps of his uncertainty with a surprise invitation for a meal for two with Sister Alfonteen. This was going to be a fact finding mission. An inquisition that would be subliminal with subtlety, Elder Standford knew it was time to use his charm.

The summer inner flower bloomed in winter for Sister Alfonteen paced through her house with a light step and a song in her heart, was Still transfixed with the Rhythm and Blues beat, she tenderised her hoover gently across the floor while cleaning the immaculate apartment of a Just, Single Woman. Memoirs inscribed in the mind, replayed in slow motion, her feelings and exquisite taste for the Standford juices of impulse surprise. She pondered, when would the next encounter be? Would he make the move for a further taste of Standford Divine, or would he be waiting for her to reciprocate with her own emotional cocktail of love and devotion. The lemon and lime seemed etched in her thoughts. Piercing through the heart of a woman's uncommon feelings of love, she wished she knew the answers to the questions that were playing through her mind. How far did he want to go with this intense new relationship? was he really serious about her or was he just a elderly sprite

Yielding (2) Temptations

man with a flair for the opposite sex?. Sister Alfonteen reasoned within herself that; Elder Standford would not approach her on two occasions `if he was not serious about his feelings of passion for her. How could he have faked the church duet dance? Sister Alfonteen concluded the Elder was genuine, looking back and reflecting on his performance and tenderness when he swept her off her feet; gave her the encouragement needed and then she never again gave it a second thought. Sister Alfonteen needed new and fresh inspiration to develop her confidence with the Elder spontaneity. How could she deal with a man that hardly reflects any emotion when in the room with other people but delivers passion in abundance when alone. Could this potential clue in the future deliver the answer she was looking for? She pondered on the previous facts of recent events.

In the cellar, the unexpected kiss of passion that flowed with milk and saliva passed through Alfonteen's body; sending a thrill of angels delight with a twist of liquored textured aftertaste with lemon on melted ice. Mints of pomegranate like juices soared through her ovaries, connecting with her hormones which were already on a high level of sexual emergency.

The unending duet of love mixed with a spiritual significance qualified Elder Standford and Sister Alfonteen to an eternal bond-ship never to be severed by human hands. While Standford swept her off her feet, her world of adventures had just begun. The eternal union blessed by being in Gods house, was witnessed by the congregation as they accepted the inevitable fact that they were meant to be together. Sister Alfonteen held the view that personal interaction with the man she loved would flourish and blossom into something that would be considered wonderful and meaningful for the future.

Yielding (2) Temptations

Alfonteen felt a completeness whenever she contemplated the interaction with her man, thoughts of him filled the void emptiness experienced throughout the tender stage of the menopause. This fulfillment was heightened by the reality of true love, manifesting itself through a fit, extremely fit elderly mature man, her mind conjured up pictures of their future togetherness, combined with, hot passionate minted unending kissing sessions which would last through the night until the sunrise. The feeling of life oozing with vitality, mixed with anticipation of internal manly connections, caressed her mind, in her 3D pictured imagination; she focused on the reality of a real man entering her vessel of welcoming love.

Love, a key word that eluded itself in the practicality of Alfonteen;s life. She thought nobody would ever love her, adore her and cherish her. The first time in her life she felt appreciated, cared for, loved and treated like a beautiful and special rose. She stood motionless in the afternoon sun, thinking about the next encounter. A positive energy began to squirm its way through her veins and made its way through her entire venous system and took over her body and set it on fire.

Elder Standford's blood was at boiling point. Hot flushes of emotion ran rampant as he clenched his fists with rage. Two Cockroaches were seen hibernating in the corner of his living room making their bed for the night. The male Cockroach had dinner brought in on a leaf to provide his partner with nutrition to produce more offspring. The Elder was not going to allow this to happen! Absolutely not. If these were the only survivors of the colony then this would mean the end of their civilization and the war would be

Yielding (2) Temptations

complete.

The lonely Cockroaches realized the new danger. After crawling through all of the known road cracks within the walls, they had ended up in this huge warm living room. The sunset was glazing through the window and the carpet was piled with a scent of lemon freshness. They felt at home, even though it was only for a brief moment. While the husband returned home bringing in new food from the kitchen, he stopped moving and was motionless as the master of the house came down hard on his wife bearing a child. The husband swung swiftly into retaliatory mode and crawled up the leg of the Cockroach Killer.

Elder Standford was not impressed. The elimination of the Cockroach with child meant nothing to him. It's guts spilled sporadically throughout the corner of the living room as Elder Standford felt an intruder inside his trouser leg. He scrimmaged and scratched his inner thigh to capture the wondering avenger. He slipped off his shoes and dragged his pants to the floor bearing all. The Cockcoach delivered an unpleasant intruder sensation within his underpants. He couldn't attack it swiftly because his testes would not allow it. He removed his briefs in the living room revealing all of his body while surveying his scrotum.

This German cockroach was going to take its revenge. Hiding in every crease and hairy scrotum, it found a tender spot when Elder Standford held his testes in his hand showing a layer of skin perfect for the German maverick Cockroach to strike and avenge the death of its wife.

Yielding (2) Temptations

Elder Standford saw the danger, and anticipating a strike; he attempted to brush off the attacker before its front legs dropped to deliver a bite in his lower genital region.

Sister "V" had decided that enough was enough. Answering the phone with a hint of attitude, Pastor "T" the 3^{rds} voice fumbled through the receiver due to "V"'s harsh and unexpected response. Pastor "T" asked if everything was ok and had she heard the latest news being networked around the congregation. Sister "V" greeted her Pastor with the reverence and the respect he deserved as a minister and proceeded by telling him that she had avoided answering her phone all day. Pastor "T" informed Sister "V" of his concerns about the sensitive nature of the Sisters in the church. Pastor "T" persuaded her to keep her eyes open and her ears to the ground while collating vital information. Sister "V" needed encouragement, spying for anybody was not her style. But in this case, she could see the advantage in helping the Pastor to make an informed decision when the time was needed. "V" indicated she will pray about the subject and confirm her decision within 48hrs. Pastor "T" had to accept this compromise and ended the call.

Yielding (2) Temptations

Next

Yielding to Temptation

Vol: II

Revelation

Yielding (2) Temptations

RELEASED!

ELUSIVE DECEPTION

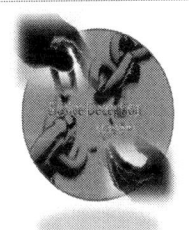

INVISIBLE CHAINS COLLECTION

The ripplings of the crescent ocean waves crashes on the shores of our known world. A cycle of the ecological processes manifesting through great intensity and fortitude, breaks through intense barriers of resistance just to complete the cycle of our continued life. Our dependency and survival relies on our planet to succeed these metamorphs of significant changes, Yet, We fail to appreciate the mesmerizing and mind blowing significance on how this natural occurrence relates to us. The co-existence of natural evolvement of society should break down the barriers of inconsistency of the mind. Yet, we emulate our reason like seasons, constantly changing throughout the courses of history. The immovability of climate social controls eludes those that need rain in a time of drought or sun through times of storm. Our harmony must be re-established if we, as a community should work together for a common cause. Synchronisation of mind, community and strength must be levelled in a racially tolerant circle of oneness; through love.

Yielding (2) Temptations

BOX OF HIDDEN SECRETS

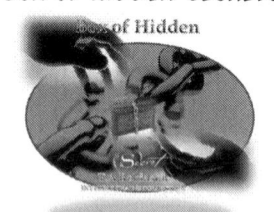

INVISIBLE CHAINS COLLECTION

The atmosphere was electrifying with every stroke of enthusiasm, the minds of the innocent became suitably engaged with the project cultured by the lecturer who was there to inspire. Minds and hearts were interwoven with the charactorial elements of Shakespeare; the literary giant of our era that had timeless masterpieces that still fills the mind with wonder. Children read out load special quotations to illuminate the intelligencier of scholarship from our ancestral past, ("I do love nothing in the world so well as you. Is not that strange?") Debates ensued with the innocent interacting with each other on the cultural differences of their meaning of "Nothing"; it brought together for a brief moment, a shared unending wealth of substantive assets, as the English Language. Dissecting and reassembling clarity through erroneous mythologies of the young, challenges the lecturer to teach invariably. To make sense of the innocent minds of his class requires stealthy wit and humorous personality to arrest the imagination of all who were in his class. Steering diligently through the potential mind-fields of dangerous thought; the curriculum personifies the way as a concealed guide to reaching absolute independence. His job will be done, if he can only but achieve this aim. A buzz with excitement was escalating as the day was coming to a close. The children wanted to learn, they were hungry to experience the rich text that would see them through life's mazes of uncertainly. They craved for the true meaning like a shinning beacon of hope and the teacher used this energy to lighten-up their personal worlds. The bell rang at a delicate moment. They wanted to stay but they had to go. There minds were widely tuned to the fount of all wisdom. The children sighed together wishing for a continuation of a second to last a little longer. They had to go...

Yielding (2) Temptations

REVELATION OF SECRETS

INVISIBLE CHAINS COLLECTION

Our illustrious past is shrouded with the mysterious intentions of the heart. The revelation through ramification of wounded souls is considered a necessary tragedy to claim a triumphant past. Great Britain has earned the stripes of causing bloodshed with a vengeance of stealing freedom from the free and chaining souls on our distant lands from remote shores. The opaque sounds of distant travellers land on an unknown territory, they take and seize possessions that they see without asking to whom they belong. White beard plunged through the dense forest looking for a purpose; they discover the free and innocent looking after their young while young mother's breast feeds their child. The evil eye of blood beard conjures up ideas which eradicates the democratic systems of primitive lands but breeds the control of ultimate authority. The white man's box of so called "tricks" fascinates the undeveloped world and influences the precious folks of those he intends to take. He uses household goods like mirrors, combs, stainless steel knives and forks to swindle the leaders of various camps to trade and release the free into prisondom. The initial responses were favourable but soon after the white men decided he needed to capture more than he could trade with and begin stealing what they have not paid for. The bludgeoning intent on pillaging the land with all its glory flourished as the slaves ships were quickly filled by the hundreds with innocent people. No mercy was shown on a free country by the visitors and the opportunity to divide and conquer was the motto replicated throughout the villages. Causing rifts and killing arch-rivals in neighbouring villages created avenues for people to be permanently kidnapped and taken over seas leaving the villagers behind blaming each other for the missing people. Wars were created as a smoke screen; for the blundering enemy was flawed as armed soldiers from the various ships were recognised as the true culprits with the missing civilians. But the British Empire continued to infiltrate and molest the guiltless to gain the trading advantages of shipping

Yielding (2) Temptations

the people abroad for personal gains. The truth with the savage reality of dissolving a man's freedom for another man's gain is the total abandonment of exercising the normal experiences of independence. The people in forceful enclave had no ideas of the tortuous adventures ahead of them, all they had were their simple assurance that God himself would deliver them from their plight. The difference in languages was an impenetrable barrier the slavers used as a tool to disassociate themselves from the groaning of the people. The battle of expressions went unheeded by the recruiters of residential hired-hands. These were scouts that knew the lands and plotted the entrapments for the prisoners to be ensnared into a lure of captivity. Slave Master's covered the regions thoroughly and engineered special search parties to gather local intelligence information for the future encounters.....

Printed in Germany
by Amazon Distribution
GmbH, Leipzig